# The Unfinished Republic

# THE UNFINISHED REPUBLIC

## *American Government in the Twenty-First Century*

KENNETH R. MLADENKA

Prentice Hall, Upper Saddle River 07458

Mladenka, Kenneth R., 1943–
   The unfinished republic : American government in the twenty-first century / Kenneth R. Mladenka.
      p.    cm.
   Includes bibliographical references and index.
   ISBN 0-13-124496-5 (pbk.)
   1. United States—Politics and government.   I. Title.
JK271.M55     1996
320.473'01—dc20                                              96-32393
                                                                CIP

Editorial Director: *Charlyce Jones Owen*
Editor-in-Chief: *Nancy Roberts*
Assistant Editor: *Jennie Katsaros*
Director of Production and Manufacturing: *Barbara Kittle*
Managing Editor: *Ann Marie McCarthy*
Project Manager: *Fran Russello*
Editorial/Production Supervision: *Publications Development Company of Texas*
Manufacturing Manager: *Nick Sklitsis*
Prepress and Manufacturing Buyer: *Bob Anderson*
Cover Design: *Bruce Kenselaar*
Director, Image Resource Center: *Lori Morris-Nantz*
Photo Research Supervisor: *Melinda Lee Reo*
Image Permission Supervisor: *Kay Dellosa*
Photo Research: *Beaura Katherine Ringrose*
Marketing Manager: *Chaun Hightower*

This book was set in 11 point Times Roman by Publications Development Company of Texas and was printed and bound by R. R. Donnelley & Sons Company. The cover was printed by Phoenix Color Corp.

© 1997, 1977, 1967 by Prentice-Hall, Inc.
Simon & Schuster/A Viacom Company
Upper Saddle River, New Jersey 07458

All rights reserved. No part of this book may be reproduced, in any form or by any means, without permission in writing from the publisher.

Printed in the United States of America
10  9  8  7  6  5  4  3  2  1

ISBN 0-13-124496-5

Prentice Hall International (UK) Limited, *London*
Prentice Hall of Australia Pty. Limited, *Sydney*
Prentice Hall Canada, Inc., *Toronto*
Prentice Hall Hispanoamericana, S.A., *Mexico*
Prentice Hall of India Private Limited, *New Delhi*
Prentice Hall of Japan, Inc., *Tokyo*
Simon & Schuster Asia Pte. Ltd., *Singapore*
Editora Prentice Hall do Brasil, Ltda., *Rio de Janeiro*

For: Linda, Brooke, Lauren, Friend, and Happy.
My favorite citizens of the Republic.

# Photo Credits

Page 3: Rick Maiman/AP/Wide World Photos
Page 4: Evan Richman/Corbis-Bettmann
Page 6: Steve & Mary Skjold/The Image Works
Page 8: Jose L. Pelaez/The Stock Market
Page 9: David Jennings/The Image Works
Page 15: Jim Mahoney/The Image Works
Page 30: The Granger Collection
Page 32: Archive Photos
Page 37: The Granger Collection
Page 44: The National Geographic Society/White House Historical Association
Page 60: Archive Photos
Page 61: National Archives
Page 68: Alan Carey/The Image Works
Page 70: Bob Daemmrich/The Image Works
Page 85: American Antiquarian Society
Page 91: Bebeto Matthews/AP/Wide World Photos
Page 92: Michael Springer/Gamma-Liaison, Inc.
Page 104: Texas Senate Media Services
Page 107: UPI/Bettmann
Page 116: John Swart/AP/Wide World Photos
Page 119: Joe Traver/Gamma-Liaison, Inc.
Page 134: UPI/Bettmann
Page 139: National Archives
Page 186: AP/Wide World Photos
Page 188: National Archives
Page 191: Hirz/Archive Photos
Page 194: Paul Conklin/PhotoEdit
Page 210: Library of Congress
Page 210: Library of Congress
Page 224: Mathew Brady/The Granger Collection
Page 230: Brady/Bettmann
Page 231: Bettmann
Page 238: Bettmann
Page 247: The Granger Collection
Page 251: UPI/Corbis-Bettmann
Page 255: Paul Conklin/PhotoEdit
Page 257: Paul Conklin/PhotoEdit
Page 266: Arnold Sachs/Uniphoto Picture Agency
Page 274: AP/Wide World Photos
Page 281: Corbis-Bettmann
Page 325: UPI/Corbis-Bettmann
Page 346: N. R. Rowan/The Image Works
Page 348: UPI/Corbis-Bettmann
Page 350: Dan Chidester/The Image Works
Page 359: Ellise Amendola/AP/Wide World Photos

# Contents

**Preface**      xv
    CONTRADICTION, CHANGE, CONSTANCY    **xv**
    PLAN OF THE BOOK    **xxiii**

**1**    *Conflict, Change, and the Future of American Politics*      1
    THE BROWNING OF AMERICA    2
    THE RISE OF THE ELDERLY    3
    ECONOMIC CHANGE    5
    A NATION OF SUBURBS    8
    THE CONFLICT OVER VALUES    11
    CRIME, VIOLENCE, AND RACE    12
        Political Impacts of Crime and Violence    14
        Two Nations: Black and White    16
    THE DECLINE OF THE NATIONAL GOVERNMENT    16
        The Federal System and Change    17
    CONCLUSION    18

**2**    *The Political Origins of the American Republic*      21
    ACCUMULATED EVILS    21
        The Common Herd    22
        Network of Dependencies    23
        The Liberation of the Common Man    24
        Mass Participation    24
    EQUALITY    25
        Classical Republicanism    26
        The Common Man and Republicanism    27
        Aristocracy of Talent    27
        Popular Government    28

ECONOMICS AND POLITICS  28
    Daniel Shays  29
    The Rebellion  31
    Alexander Hamilton  31
STATE LEGISLATURES  34
    Radical Democracy  35
    Radical Laws  35
DIRECT DEMOCRACY  36
ELITE FEARS  36

## 3 The Constitution     40

THE OPENING SHOT  43
MADISON TAKES THE OFFENSIVE  43
THE REACTION  44
THE CONSTITUTION TAKES SHAPE  45
IDEALISM OR ECONOMICS  46
ECONOMIC POWERS  48
SOMETHING FOR EVERYONE  48
MILITARY POWERS  49
NATIONAL SUPREMACY  50
IN DEFENSE OF THE FRAMERS  50
THE IMPORTANCE OF PROPERTY  52
THE FEDERALIST, NO. 10  53
MAINTAINING THE SPIRIT AND FORM  54
RATIFICATION  55
ANTIFEDERALISTS  57
    Antifederalist Criticisms  57
THE STATE CONVENTIONS  58
NEW YORK  62
THE LEGACY OF RATIFICATION  63
CONCLUSION  63

## 4 Federalism     66

CHANGE AND FEDERALISM  66
FEDERAL SYSTEMS  67
    The Advantages of Federalism  68
    Disadvantages of Federalism  71
STATE AND NATIONAL POWERS  72
    Court Decisions  73
    Amendments  75
    Money  76
STAGES OF FEDERALISM  77

CHALLENGES TO FEDERALISM  83
THE ULTIMATE CHALLENGE  86
THE FUTURE OF FEDERALISM  87

## 5  Interest Groups and Political Parties    89

CHANGE AND INTEREST GROUPS  89
CHANGE AND THE PARTY SYSTEM  90
INTEREST GROUPS GAIN POWER  92
    The Indians Win Again  92
    The Gospel According to Ralph  93
THE FUNCTIONS OF INTEREST GROUPS  93
CRITICISMS OF INTEREST GROUPS  95
    Labor as an Interest Group—A Case Study  95
RESOURCES  99
PUBLIC PERCEPTIONS OF INTEREST GROUPS  101
INTEREST GROUP TACTICS  102
    Lobbying  102
    Efforts to Control Lobbyists  103
    Electioneering  103
    Public Relations Campaigns  106
    Protest Demonstrations  106
    Women as an Interest Group—A Long and Winding Road  108
    The Environment and Interest Groups  109
    New Groups on the Block  112
    Conclusion  113
POLITICAL PARTIES  113
    The Functions of Political Parties  113
    The Decline of Political Parties  114
    Party Identification  115
    Republican Growth  115
    Group Identification  116
    Ideological Unity  116
    Third Parties  117
    Party Organization  118
    A Decentralized Party System  120
CONCLUSION  121

## 6  Political Minorities    123

NATIVE AMERICANS  124
    The West  127
BLACKS  136
    A Brief History  136
    The Reaction  141

Poverty and Welfare **143**
Income **144**
Jobs **145**
White Myths/Black Truths **149**
HISPANICS **150**
Mexican-Americans **153**
Puerto Ricans **157**
Cubans **157**
WOMEN **159**
GAYS **169**
CONCLUSION **170**

## 7 *The Political Economy* 172

THE POLITICAL CONSEQUENCES OF CURRENT
ECONOMIC CHANGE **175**
POLITICS, ECONOMIC SELF-INTEREST, AND THE BIRTH OF
THE NATION **176**
TO BUILD A NATION **178**
INDUSTRIALIZATION **179**
The Progressives **180**
The Populists **182**
Uneven Development in the North and South **182**
Political Effects of Uneven Economic Development **183**
Scientific Management **184**
THE EMERGENCE OF THE MODERN CORPORATE STATE **185**
THE GREAT DEPRESSION **185**
The Political Response to the Great Depression **187**
Political Impacts **188**
THE IMPACT OF POLITICS UPON ECONOMICS **190**
WORLD WAR II **190**
LABOR, BUSINESS, AND POLITICS **191**
COMPETING POLITICAL PERSPECTIVES ON
THE ECONOMY **192**
THE GOVERNMENT AND THE ECONOMY **192**
Federal Reserve System **193**
Regulation of the Economy **195**
Deregulation **196**
CONCLUSION **197**

## 8 *The Presidency* 199

THE CHANGING PRESIDENCY **199**
THE TITLE **201**

THE CONVENTION   201
THE ROAD TO THE WHITE HOUSE   204
POWERS, ORGANIZATION, FUNCTIONS   206
    Powers   206
    The Cabinet   210
    Impeachment   210
    Amendments   212
    Veto Power   212
    Executive Office of the Presidency   213
    White House Staff   214
THE PRESIDENT'S WAR POWERS   214
PRESIDENTIAL FRUSTRATIONS   222
THE BEST AND THE WORST   226
PRESIDENTIAL PERFORMANCE   234
PUBLIC OPINION   236
CONCLUSION   243

## 9   *Congress*    245

CONGRESS AND CHANGE   245
THE IDEA BEHIND CONGRESS   247
THE POWERS OF CONGRESS   250
QUALIFICATIONS FOR OFFICE   252
THE ORGANIZATION OF CONGRESS   252
    Leadership in the House   252
    Leadership in the Senate   254
    The Committee System   254
HOW A BILL BECOMES A LAW   258
WHY THEY VOTE AS THEY DO   262
CONGRESS AND THE PRESIDENT   265
CONGRESSIONAL OVERSIGHT   267

## 10   *The Judiciary and Civil Liberties*    270

AT THE CREATION   271
    The Judiciary Act of 1789   272
THE EARLY COURT   273
THE MARSHALL COURT   273
THE ORGANIZATION AND STRUCTURE OF THE
    FEDERAL JUDICIARY   277
    District Courts   277
    Courts of Appeal   277
    The Supreme Court   278
    The Solicitor General   279

　　　　　Deciding the Case   **283**
　　　　　Judicial Decisions and Implementation   **284**
　　　　　*Brown v. Board of Education* and Implementation   **287**
　　　　　The Selection of Judges   **289**
　　　　　Appointments to the Supreme Court   **290**
　　　　　Senate Confirmation   **290**
　　　　　Characteristics of Current Supreme Court Justices   **292**
　　　CIVIL LIBERTIES   **292**
　　　　　First Amendment Freedoms   **292**
　　　　　The Free Exercise Clause   **297**
　　　　　Freedom of Expression   **298**
　　　　　Does the Bill of Rights Apply to State and
　　　　　　　Local Governments?   **298**
　　　　　Symbolic Speech   **299**
　　　　　Libel   **300**
　　　　　Pornography and Obscenity   **300**
　　　　　Freedom of Expression and the "Clear and Present
　　　　　　　Danger" Test   **301**
　　　　　Another Contradiction—Freedom of the Press versus the Rights
　　　　　　　of Defendants   **302**
　　　　　The Right of the People Peaceably to Assemble   **302**
　　　　　Criminal Rights   **303**
　　　　　Self-Incrimination and the Fifth Amendment   **304**
　　　　　The Right to Counsel and the Sixth Amendment   **304**
　　　　　Trial by Jury and the Sixth Amendment   **305**
　　　　　Cruel and Unusual Punishment   **306**
　　　　　Privacy and the Bill of Rights   **306**

**11**　*Bureaucracy*　　　　　　　　　　　　　　　　　　　　　　　　　　**309**
　　　HISTORICAL DEVELOPMENT   **311**
　　　BUREAUCRATIC CHARACTERISTICS   **314**
　　　BUREAUCRATIC DECISION MAKING   **315**
　　　THE CONTRADICTIONS OF BUREAUCRACY   **318**
　　　　　Fairness versus Responsiveness   **318**
　　　　　Efficiency versus Effectiveness   **319**
　　　　　Independence versus Accountability   **319**
　　　SOURCES OF BUREAUCRATIC POWER   **320**
　　　LIMITS ON BUREAUCRATIC POWER   **322**
　　　　　Professional Norms   **322**
　　　　　Incrementalism   **322**
　　　　　Media   **323**
　　　　　Congress   **323**

**Contents** xiii

    The President 326
    The Freedom of Information Act 327
    Federalism 327
  THE ORGANIZATION OF THE BUREAUCRACY 328
    The Cabinet Departments 328
    Government Corporations 329
    Regulatory Commissions 330
    Independent Agencies 331
  REGULATION AND CAPTURE 331
  CITIZEN PERCEPTIONS OF THE BUREAUCRACY 334
  POLITICAL REPRESENTATION 337
  SUMMARY 339

**12** *Public Opinion, Participation, Nominations and Campaigns, Elections, the Media* 343
  PUBLIC OPINION 343
    Polls 344
    The Impact of Polling 344
    Political Ideology and Public Opinion 345
  PARTICIPATION 347
    Voting 349
    Contacting 350
    Group Activity 351
    Nonviolent Protest 352
    Violence 354
    Exit 356
    The Effectiveness of Political Participation 357
  NOMINATIONS, CAMPAIGNS, AND ELECTIONS 358
    Nominations 358
    Campaigns 361
    Elections 364
  THE MEDIA 367

*Index* 371

# About the Author

Kenneth R. Mladenka received a Ph.D. from Rice University in 1975 and taught for 20 years as a professor of political science at the University of Virginia, Northwestern University, and Texas A&M University. His research on American politics has been published in the *American Political Science Review, Journal of Politics, American Journal of Political Science, Social Science Quarterly, Wilson Quarterly,* and *Urban Affairs Quarterly.* Shortly after graduating from college, he served in Vietnam (1967–1968) as a platoon leader with the Fourth Infantry Division.

# Acknowledgments

I owe a large debt of gratitude to Jennie Katsaros, my editor at Prentice Hall. She was everything a good editor should be—insightful, supportive, and diligent. I would also like to thank the anonymous reviewers who were always supportive and constructive in their criticism of the manuscript. This is a better book because of them. Appreciation is also expressed to Nancy Houston who did a marvelous job of typing the manuscript, and to Nancy Marcus Land and her staff at Publications Development Company of Texas who did an excellent job of editing and preparing the manuscript for publication. Finally, I am deeply and eternally grateful to my wife Linda. As you know, it is not always easy living with a political scientist—particularly one writing a book. She accomplishes the task with a remarkable degree of humor, tolerance, and compassion.

# *Preface*

## CONTRADITION, CHANGE, CONSTANCY

### Contradiction

The American Republic was fraught with powerful contradictions and enduring ironies from the very beginning. Abraham Lincoln would proclaim at Gettysburg in 1863 that "four score and seven years ago the founders had brought forth on the continent a new nation, conceived in liberty and dedicated to the proposition that all men are created equal." But there was not a single mention of the words equal or equality in the Constitution, and it required Lincoln's own powerful legacy to graft the Fourteenth Amendment to the Constitution after both Lincoln and the Civil War had passed. The nation may have been conceived in liberty, but no less a member of the revolutionary elite than Richard Henry Lee of Virginia could look at the just completed Constitution and find it "really astonishing that the same people who have just emerged from a long and cruel war in defense of liberty, should now agree to fix an elective despotism upon themselves and their posterity."[1]

A powerful contradiction existed between elitism and egalitarianism. The decade of the Constitution was a period of deep disillusionment for many of the revolutionary leaders. These "first generation gentlemen" had envisioned a republic founded on the willingness of its citizens to place the public interest above narrow self-interest. Leadership for this virtuous republic would be drawn from the ranks of an "aristocracy of talent." Membership would be determined not by blood, kinship, or social standing, but by genius and merit. Promising young men would receive a liberal education, acquire an "enlightened" character, and thereby properly equip themselves for admittance to the

---

[1] Quoted in Gordon S. Wood, *The Radicalism of the American Revolution* (New York: Knopf, 1992).

ranks of the elite. But just as the Revolution had challenged and transformed existing patterns of political and social authority, so the Revolution unleashed other powerful forces as well. As we will see in Chapter 2, one of these powerful forces was egalitarianism. Ordinary Americans came to think that they were as good as everyone else. More importantly, they came to act that way. They came to believe that they were capable of self-government, and that government existed to help them obtain their private ends.

According to this perspective, the people were the ultimate source of political authority. Several developments during this period—the radicalization of state legislatures; citizen participation through the mechanisms of conventions, committees, and associations; the enactment of legislation in several states providing for debtor relief and the issuance of paper currency; and Shays' Rebellion—were interpreted by the elite as assaults on liberty and property.[2] The people apparently were as capable of despotism as any prince. James Madison came to see that the few had much more to fear from the many, than the many had to fear from the few. This growing alarm over the tyranny of the majority was aggravated by the low regard in which the elite held the masses. George Washington referred to them as "the grazing multitude," John Adams described them as the "Common Herd of Mankind," and Governor Morris characterized them as "Poor reptiles! They bask in the sun, and ere noon they will bite, depend upon it." Poor prospects indeed upon which to pin posterity's hopes for republican government. The framers' solution to the problem of a lack of political virtue among the people was an ingenious one. Entrust the future of republican government to the new institutions created by the Constitution rather than to the virtue of the people.

Only some of the powerful contradictions that had plagued the American Republic from its origins would be resolved by the Civil War. The issue of the contingent nature of the Union was settled with a striking finality. No longer would individual states (South Carolina during the nullification crisis), or groups of states (New England during the War of 1812), threaten secession. Before the Civil War, the nation was referred to as "The United States are . . ." Afterwards, it became, "The United States is . . ." The bane of slavery had also been eradicated, its deadly poison leached by violence from the political fabric of the Republic.

But other issues defied resolution. Conflicts over the power of the states versus that of the national government would dominate the post-war evolution of the federal system. State resistance to the imposition of a national policy agenda—in conjunction with the lingering effects of the Reconstruction Era—would produce a pattern of highly uneven political and social development among the states. Within this context, the continuing struggle and halting

---

[2] Wood, *Radicalism of the American Revolution*.

progress of various minorities would come to represent one of the great ironies of American self-government. The tortuous path followed by African Americans, Native Americans, women, ethnic minorities, and Hispanics in their quest for a measure of the political, social, and economic equality promised them by the American dream would prove to be an enduring contradiction throughout the nation's history.

A connecting tissue among the chapters is provided by the importance of often contradictory beliefs and ideas in the development of the American political system. It was the belief in classical republican values that served as one of the most basic foundations for the emerging nation. In turn, the growing power and appeal of egalitarianism—in combination with the increasing likelihood of ordinary citizens to participate directly in political affairs—clashed with elitist notions of a virtuous republic led by gentlemen drawn from an "aristocracy of talent." It was the conflict generated by competing beliefs regarding the issues of sovereignty, direct democracy, representation, interests, leadership, and the appropriate nature and ends of public power, that defined the constitutional era.

Another idea that powerfully shaped American politics was the belief in divine inspiration and guidance. The Puritans believed that just as God had driven out the tribes of Canaan for the benefit of the Israelites, so God would drive out the Indians. John Winthrop knew that the "God of Israel is among us." When an epidemic decimated the Indian population in 1633 he observed, "If God were not pleased with our inheriting these parts, why did he drive the natives before us?" Three hundred and fifty years later, Ronald Reagan would proclaim, "I have always believed that this anointed land was set apart in an uncommon way, that a divine plan placed this great continent here between the oceans." President Woodrow Wilson, son of a Presbyterian minister, professor of government, and president of Princeton University, wrote that "America was born a Christian nation; America was born to exemplify that devotion to the elements of righteousness which are derived from the revelation of Holy Scripture."

Racism was another powerful doctrine that spawned its own set of contradictions. President Andrew Jackson asked in 1830, "What good man would prefer a country covered with forests and ranged by a few thousand savages to our extensive Republic . . . occupied by more than 12,000,000 happy people and filled with the blessing of liberty, civilization, and religion?" Alexis de Tocqueville observed that white Americans "scarcely acknowledge the common features of humanity in this stranger whom slavery has brought among them." He predicted that "the abolition of slavery will increase the repugnance of the white population for the blacks."[3] *The Cincinnati Enquirer* editorialized

---

[3] Alexis de Tocqueville, *Democracy in America* (New York: Mentor Books, 1956).

at the end of the Civil War that "slavery is dead, the negro is not, there is the misfortune." Intellectuals labored to lend a patina of scientific respectability to racist beliefs. Some, such as Louis Agassig of Harvard University, maintained that whites were genetically superior. The doctrine of Social Darwinism, created by the Englishman Herbert Spencer and propagated in America by William Graham Sumner of Yale University, argued for the legitimacy of the strong dominating the weak by virtue of the inevitability of survival of the fittest.

When the concept of Americans as a "chosen people" merged with a belief in racial superiority, a powerful hybrid was born. In 1874, Samuel Harris, professor of Theology at Yale University, proclaimed that it was to the Anglo-Saxon race "more than any other that the world is now indebted for the propagation of Christian Civilization." James King, a Protestant clergyman, observed that God had chosen the Anglo-Saxons "to conquer the world for Christ by dispossessing feeble races, and assimilating and molding others." Josiah Strong, another influential clergyman, thought that eventually all of mankind would be "Anglo-Saxonized."

It would not take long for this new nation, where the people saw themselves as "chosen" by God, to come to believe themselves invincible in battle. John Winthrop proclaimed that with the "God of Israel among us . . . ten of us shall be able to resist a thousand of our enemies." Oliver Wendell Holmes believed that the message of war was "divine."[4] President Woodrow Wilson acknowledged no contradiction between political violence and Christian principles. It was clear to him that "When men take up arms to set other men free, there is something sacred and holy in warfare. I will not cry 'peace' as long as there is sin and wrong in the world." Increasingly, America's wars became religious crusades. Religion's warriors marched to the song, "Onward Christian Soldiers." According to the "Battle Hymn of the Republic," the nation's soldiers had a mission even more important than Christ's. While Jesus died "to make men holy," Americans died "to make men free." When President Wilson returned from the peace conference in France at the end of World War I, he proclaimed, "At last the world knows America as the savior of the world." America had become Godlike.

Several powerful and often contradictory beliefs shaped the nation's behavior both at home and abroad throughout much of its history: Republicanism, egalitarianism, divine guidance, racial superiority, and invincibility on the field of battle. Together, they provided the basis for a potent national ideology. Perhaps no one ever more clearly expressed that ideology than Senator Albert Beveridge of Indiana who, in a speech supporting the American war against the

---

[4] Richard Severo and Lewis Millford, *The Wages of War* (New York: Simon & Schuster, 1989).

Philippines—a war in which 16,000 guerrillas and 100,000 civilians died—observed that,

> We will not renounce our part in the mission of our race but will move forward to our work . . . with gratitude for a task worthy of our strength and thanksgiving to Almighty God that He has marked us as His chosen people, henceforth to lead in the regeneration of the world. And of all our race He has marked the American people as His chosen nation. . . . This is the divine mission of America, and it holds for us all the profit, all the glory, all the happiness possible to man. We are trustees of the world's progress, guardians of its righteous peace.[5]

But mixed in with these powerful beliefs in the superiority and invincibility of the American nation was also a genuine sense of idealism (what Lincoln called "the better angels of our nature"). The God who smiled upon the Puritans in their violent subjugation of the Indians would also inspire and sustain the Abolitionists in their unrelenting attacks on the evils of slavery. Enormously proud of her political, social, and economic institutions, America would be moved by that same sense of idealism to bestow the blessings conferred by God's Grace and Divine Providence upon others. America's growing involvement in the international arena during the twentieth century would profoundly alter the course of human history.

Another contradiction exists between what the American Republic promises and what it delivers. Our political tradition abounds with eloquent, powerful, and stirring appeals to the dispossessed and downtrodden: "All men are created equal," "conceived in liberty," "life, liberty, and the pursuit of happiness," "government of the people, by the people, and for the people." However, resistance to demands for a larger measure of political and economic justice for minorities has been given up only grudgingly.

Powerful and contradictory beliefs have shaped America's political destiny. These contradictions are as much a part of the Republic's political life today as they were in the eighteenth and nineteenth centuries. As a people, we are still confronted with the contradictions between egalitarianism and elitism, between the search for social justice and the demands of economic efficiency, between Christian brotherhood and racial superiority, between secularism and the belief in divine guidance, between tolerance and bigotry, between fairness and survival of the fittest, between individualism and the longing for community, between the myth of the melting pot and the reality of isolated racial and class enclaves.

It is this theme of contradiction that will be emphasized in the pages that follow. These contradictions have structured and shaped the nature of political

---

[5] Forrest G. Wood, *The Arrogance of Faith* (New York: Harper & Row, 1990).

conflict in America, and our political institutions and processes have evolved in an effort to resolve them. Some of the nation's most powerful contradictions have been ignored. Others have been confronted with considerably less than satisfactory results. The enduring promise of the Republic is that each generation will try anew.

## Change

Change is a major focus of this book. The country is undergoing enormous change, and the consequences of those transformations will permanently alter the American political system. For example, demographic shifts will exert profound effects on the distribution of power in society. The time is approaching when a majority of Americans will be nonwhite. The extraordinary political consequences of these population changes will be examined in an effort to help understand the political future of the country. The "browning" of America is already evident. In New York state, 40 percent of the children enrolled in the public schools are nonwhite. In California, the figure is 51 percent. In San Jose, the Nguyens outnumber the Jones in the phone directory—fourteen columns to eight. A multiracial and multicultural society will produce enormous political strains and tensions. This country has had past experience with demographic change, but the great waves of ethnic migration in the nineteenth and the first part of the twentieth century were different in one fundamental respect: The new arrivals were white.

We already see indications of the heightened tension these demographic transformations are likely to produce. One ominous sign is a rise in the incidence of racial discrimination and instances of racially motivated violence and brutality. In the classroom, there are conflicts over bilingual education and multicultural curriculum. Grievances and discontent may increase if African Americans perceive that the increased political and economic power enjoyed by Hispanics and Asians has been obtained at their expense. Potential interracial conflict may incorporate an element of intergenerational tension as well. As the white population ages, an increasing number of retirees will be supported by a heavily nonwhite working population. The opportunities for enhanced political tension in such an environment are enormous.

Some predictions hold that by the middle of the next century, America will already be a majority nonwhite society. For the first time in a history spanning 400 years, the nation will be forced to accept the reality of a society no longer dominated by white beliefs, biases, and myths. Already, the Republic is beginning to engage in the agonizing reappraisal of what it will mean to be a citizen of the Republic when African, Hispanic, and Asian Americans will wield the political, cultural, and social influence that defines a society's most basic institutions, values, and beliefs.

The fundamental economic changes that are sweeping the country and the world will also exert profound effects upon the nation's political future. The globalization of the economy, the shift from an industrial to an information processing and high-tech economy, and the growing challenges to America's economic position in the international arena, will combine to substantially alter the domestic political fabric. For example, if the pattern of redistributing wealth from the rich to the poor continues, we can anticipate the eventual likelihood of heightened class conflict. A high-tech economy may also entail significant political consequences. Some believe that such an economy will produce a small group of highly paid professionals and managers and a very large group of marginally rewarded clerks, secretaries, fast-food workers, and janitors. The former group will reap enormous rewards from the system; the latter group will suffer underemployment, low wages, and little opportunity for advancement. A high-tech economy may cause a shrinking of the middle class and the further erosion of labor union membership. One possible outcome is a redistribution of political power as well as increased class polarization.

Economic change in the United States has always caused profound political change. The transformation of the economy from an agricultural to an industrial base in the late nineteenth and early twentieth centuries radically altered social and political relationships. Great cities developed as people moved from rural to urban areas. The ethnic and religious composition of the country changed as a result of a massive influx of immigrants from abroad. Political power was redistributed as labor unions began to organize, the middle class grew, and blacks migrated from the South to Midwestern and Northeastern cities. This economic transformation also caused broad movements of political protest, beginning with the Populists and Progressives. The size and scope of government dramatically expanded as more programs and services were required by an increasingly complex society. The power and role of the bureaucracy grew as government assumed responsibility for regulating a wide array of social and economic activities.

The enormous and enduring success of the American political experiment could not have been accomplished and sustained without the limitless energy and vast resources created by a powerful economic engine. The prodigious industrial capacity and awesome technological prowess of the Republic helped propel the American people to the very center of the world stage. Politics and economics are so powerfully intertwined that careful attention will be given the role of the latter in the political origins, evolution, and maturity of the American political system.

## Constancy

The history of the nation is rich, colorful, and exciting—full of rogues and idealists, scoundrels and saints. Each generation produced statesmen, visionaries, religious fanatics, profiteers, corrupt politicians, warlords and warmongers, pacifists, crusaders, martyrs, and great writers, explorers, and inventors.

America's political history is written in successive waves of fervor and passion and violence. The history of the country is an exciting adventure. The extraordinary energy, determination, and endurance of the early Americans allowed them to settle the wilderness and conquer the Indians. They fought a war for independence, invented a Republic, and established and defended the legitimacy of the nation. They created a flourishing society in one great region of the country based on slave labor, fought a bitter and horrendous war to destroy that slave economy, and in the process redefined American democracy. They reacted to the profound changes wrought by industrialization and immigration by forming vast waves of political protest—Populism and Progressivism. The country grew prosperous and powerful, flexed its muscles in the international arena, pursued imperialistic interests abroad, and fought a great war in Europe. The Depression dealt a glancing blow to unbridled capitalism and gravely challenged national self-confidence. The country restored both its prosperity and self-esteem in World War II and emerged from that conflict as the world's dominant military and economic power—as well as its policeman. The next half century would witness a superpower confrontation with the Soviets during the Cold War, the threat of nuclear annihilation, the communist witch hunts and paranoia of the McCarthy era, the Civil Rights movement, the Kennedy assassination, the agony and despair of Vietnam, the shame of Watergate, the deterioration of America's economy, the Reagan years, and the patriotic rejuvenation of the Gulf War.

An understanding of the historical development of the country also provides a sound basis for an understanding of America's political present and future. American politics is characterized by historical cycles. During certain periods in the country's history, the national public agenda is dominated by a concern with economic productivity and efficiency. At other times, this emphasis is displaced by a focus on social equity and justice issues which, in turn, eventually gives away to a preoccupation with a law-and-order agenda. Each new cycle of public priorities produces a different set of political policies, outcomes, and impact. An emphasis upon political history, therefore, not only enhances readability but provides the student with the basis for evaluating America's political present and future.

The significance of individual Americans will also be emphasized. What if, by the mere accident of birth, the revolutionary generation had been absent the following six men: Thomas Jefferson, George Washington, James Madison, John Adams, Alexander Hamilton, and John Marshall? What if Nat Turner had never heard the voice of God commanding him to lead his bloody slave rebellion in 1831, or if John Brown had not heard the same voice at Harper's Ferry 28 years later? What if Harriet Beecher Stowe had not grown dissatisfied with being a wife and mother to her seven children and had never written *Uncle Tom's Cabin,* if Abraham Lincoln had not been elected to the presidency where

*Preface* xxiii

he would preserve the Union and redefine American democracy, or if John Wilkes Booth had not heeded the counsel of his own personal demons to murder Lincoln? What if "Tailgunner" Joe McCarthy had never lived to invent the political movement of hysteria that bears his name?

American society offers a high standard of living; immense opportunity and reward for many; vast personal freedom; relatively honest, open, and efficient government; substantial progress in civil rights; and an opportunity to share in the national largess and reap the rewards of full citizenship. The opportunities and rewards that are so eagerly offered to some are summarily denied to others. America at its best sets standards that are exceedingly high. The Declaration of Independence, the Gettysburg Address, and Martin Luther King's "I Have a Dream" speech eloquently affirmed the national political ideal and purpose for their respective centuries. With ends that are so noble, the nature of the nation's means as well as the reality of her accomplishments frequently suffers by comparison. One thing is certain: Every significant political development advances the dreams of some Americans; every significant political development defers the dreams of others. As the Republic enters its next century, whose dreams will be realized? Whose dreams will be deferred?

## PLAN OF THE BOOK

The related themes of contradiction, constancy, and change guide this book. The powerful and enduring contradictions of the American political experience (republicanism, egalitarianism, elitism, racism, divine guidance) provide a connecting thread between the chapters. In Chapter 2 (Political Origins of the American Republic) and Chapter 3 (Constitution), we will trace the decisive conflicts over control of the Republic's political future between the elites ("propertied gentlemen of virtue") and those ordinary citizens who had become imbued with the spirit of egalitarianism unleashed during the Revolutionary era ("reptiles basking in the sun," according to their elitist opponents).

In Chapter 6 (Political Minorities), we will witness the bitter political conflicts generated by the clash between the quest for equality on the one hand, and the powerful forces of racism on the other. These forces—deeply ingrained in the political fabric of the American experience—are illustrated by the horrible and chilling words of Roger B. Taney, Chief Justice of the United States Supreme Court, who proclaimed that black Americans were "so far inferior, that they had no rights which the white man was bound to respect; and that the negro [therefore] might justly and lawfully be reduced to slavery for his benefit." The powerful national contradiction between egalitarianism and racism is further illustrated by the same Chief Justice who, as an advocate of Jacksonian Democracy, wrote that "every man is equally entitled to protection by law."

The frequently contradictory nature of the nation's political beliefs will be emphasized throughout the book. In Chapter 8 on the presidency, for example, we will see that several of the nation's presidents often reflected the larger society's ambivalence and contradictions regarding racial superiority, Christian principles of brotherhood and pacifism, and sense of military invincibility. No president better illustrated these contradictions than Woodrow Wilson—one of the best educated and most scholarly of all the nation's Chief Executives. He could sincerely profess the universal equality and Christian brotherhood of all men. He could also practice discrimination against black federal employees, treat women as intellectually inferior, and resist efforts to enfranchise women despite the repeated entreaties of his daughters. He could dedicate his life and that of the nation to Christian principles, and yet advocate war and violence to achieve his goals. He could believe in the dignity of all mankind, while also insisting that God had selected Americans as His "Chosen People" to deliver salvation and democracy to inferior races throughout the world.

The second theme is change. In Chapter 1, we examine several significant changes that will exert an impact upon the American political system. These include the aging of the population, demographic change, economic upheaval, suburbanization, the cultural conflict over values, race and violence, and the decline of national power. The chapters on Political Economy, the Presidency, Congress, Judiciary, and Interest Groups and Political Parties consider how these changes are likely to influence political institutions and processes. The intent is to get students to think critically about American government and politics in dynamic rather than static terms.

The third theme is constancy, what Abraham Lincoln in his First Inaugural Address called "the mystic chords of memory." A shared historical experience holds the nation together, just as the forces of change tend to pull it apart. These "mystic chords of memory"—the Revolutionary period, slavery, the Civil War, Reconstruction, the Progressive era, immigration, the World Wars, the Depression, the Civil Rights movement, Vietnam—will be examined from the perspective of how the nation's political history illuminates the present and perhaps even suggests the contours of the future. For example, conflicts between the elites and ordinary American citizens during the Revolutionary era—as illustrated in our portraits of Alexander Hamilton and Daniel Shays—are clearly relevant to understanding the political conflicts between elites and masses today. Similarly, portraits of various presidents are used to demonstrate the enormous pressures, frustrations, and opportunities historically associated with the position.

These three themes—constancy, contradiction, and change—connect the chapters. An understanding of the political past helps in our effort to grasp the meaning and purpose of the present. A recognition of the powerful contradictions embedded in the political and social fabric of the nation—egalitarianism and elitism, the yearning for social justice and fairness on the one hand and the incessant striving for economic success and survival of the fittest on the other, Christian principles and racial superiority, secularism and divine guidance, "rugged" individualism and the longing for community and purpose—helps us understand why public officials find it so exceedingly difficult to discover and serve the "public interest." And finally, an examination of change permits us to glimpse—if only dimly—the emerging shape of the nation's political future.

Kenneth R. Mladenka

# 1

# *Conflict, Change, and the Future of American Politics*

The Browning of America
The Rise of the Elderly
Economic Change
A Nation of Suburbs
The Conflict over Values

Crime, Violence, and Race
   *Political Impacts of Crime and Violence*
   *Two Nations: Black and White*
The Decline of the National Government
   *The Federal System and Change*
Conclusion

> What then is the American, this new man?
> —Hector St. John de Crevecoeur, Eighteenth century

> Here is not merely a nation, but a teaming nation of nations.
> —Walt Whitman

In this chapter, I will point out the enormous changes that are taking place in American society, emphasize how these changes translate into political conflict, and analyze how our governmental institutions and processes both deal with and adapt to these changes. This is not an easy task. The contours and content of these changes can be only dimly perceived. But to ignore the future because we cannot see it would be to acknowledge that the nation's government and politics can be understood and experienced only as history. To do that would be foolhardy. As individuals, we know these changes are already unfolding. We are forced to deal with them in our personal lives. To ignore them in the political life of the nation until after they have passed into the historical record would be to forfeit the opportunity to understand these changes as they are unfolding.

We have identified these changes as:

- *The Browning of America;*
- *The Rise of the Elderly;*
- *Economic Change;*
- *A Nation of Suburbs;*
- *The Conflict over Values;*
- *Crime, Violence, and Race;* and
- *The Decline of the National Government.*

## THE BROWNING OF AMERICA

Although its ultimate impact will not be realized for another fifty years, one of the most profound changes in the history of the nation is already taking place. America is changing color. By the middle of the next century, the "average" American will trace his or her descent to Africa, Asia, Arabia, or the Hispanic world. Estimates are that the number of immigrants—both legal and illegal—entering the country will total 880,000 each year for the next sixty years, and could reach as high as 1.4 million a year. By 2050, the population may well include 100 million people who arrived in the United States after 1991, or were born to parents who did. Demographers predict that while the white population will stop growing by 2029, the black population will double by 2050 to 62 million, the Asian population will reach 41 million by 2050, and the Hispanic population will more than triple to 81 million.

Two sources will fuel the dramatic growth in the nonwhite population during the next fifty years. The first is immigration. Two-thirds of all the immigration in the world consists of people coming to the United States. The second is birth rates. Between 1980 and 1990, the white population in the country grew by 3 percent. During the same period, the black population grew by 13 percent, the Hispanic population by 34 percent, and the Asian population by 56 percent. Already, the effects of this racial transformation are being felt. Several major American cities have a majority nonwhite population. Fifteen out of 16 black and Hispanic students in these big cities attend schools where few whites are enrolled. The Los Angeles County court system provides interpreters for eighty different languages, ranging from Albanian and Amharic to Turkish and Tongan. On the 1990 census form, Americans used a write-in category to identify themselves as belonging to 300 races or ethnic groups, 75 combinations of multiracial ancestry, 70 different Hispanic groups, and 600 different Indian tribes. In 1970, there were 310,000 interracial married couples. That number had almost quadrupled by 1993 to 1,195,000. The Dade

New Americans take the oath of allegiance. (Credit: AP Laser Photo)

County, Florida, school district—the fourth largest in the nation—includes students from 123 countries.

Racial change will likely have enormous political consequences. For the first time in the history of the nation—a history spanning 400 years—white Americans will find themselves a minority rather than the majority. Challenges to traditional values—in areas such as English as the official language, affirmative action, the content of the classroom curriculum, and the distribution of power and authority in society—are already taking place. These challenges, and the political conflict that develops as a result, will intensify as the browning of America continues. As we will see, the racial transformation of the nation will also complicate the resolution of a number of other divisive political issues.

## THE RISE OF THE ELDERLY

Today, Americans over the age of 65 account for 13 percent of the population. However, they consume more than one-third of all health-care spending. The elderly fill 40 percent of all the hospital beds in the nation and use twice as much prescription medication as all other Americans combined. Even though the elderly constitute a small proportion of the total population, they have had a major impact on national spending. Support of the elderly has surpassed defense spending as the most expensive federal program. Social Security and Medicare account for more than $500 billion in a budget of $1.5 trillion.

The Congressional Budget Office reports that in 1965 Social Security and Medicare costs accounted for 14 percent of the federal spending, while defense accounted for 43 percent. By 1995, however, defense spending had dramatically declined to only 18 percent of federal budget expenditures, while Social Security and Medicare costs had dramatically jumped to 34 percent. The problem will only get worse. In 10 years, it is projected that defense spending will further decline to 16 percent of the federal budget. By 2005, however, Social Security and Medicare costs will consume almost 40 percent of all federal spending.

The total cost of caring for the elderly will dramatically increase in the coming decades. Some demographers predict that there may be as many as 138 million Americans over the age of 65 by 2040. Significantly, the number of citizens 85 years and older—currently 3.3 million—will climb to 6.5 million by the year 2020. Projections are that this number will soar to 17.7 million by the middle of the century, while the number of people 100 years old and older (now at 45,000) will rise to more than one million by 2050. Other demographic forecasts conclude that the number of Americans over the age of 65 will actually climb to a figure much higher than this. These "oldest old"—people 85 years and older—account for twice as much spending for healthcare as the merely elderly. Since the oldest old are growing at an even faster rate than the rest of the elderly population, we can anticipate an astronomical increase in the proportion of national resources devoted to care for the elderly.

The dramatic increase in the number of elderly Americans will impose enormous financial stress upon the nation in another

Marathon runners John Kelley (77) and Ruth Rothfarb (84). (Credit: UPI/Corbis-Bettmann)

way as well. Most social security recipients today use up every dollar they paid into the system, plus interest, within their first six years of retirement. When the social security program began, there were forty-six workers contributing their tax dollars for every citizen drawing benefits. By the time the current baby boomer population retires, only two workers will be contributing to the program for every beneficiary.

The implications are astounding. First, the dramatic increase in the elderly population will test the fiscal capacity of the nation through spiraling social security and health-care costs. Second, the stage will be set for a series of potentially bitter and divisive political conflicts between a heavily nonwhite and youthful working population that pays the taxes, and a heavily white and elderly population that receives the benefits. Already, elderly Americans are well-organized politically. Established in 1958, the American Association of Retired Persons now claims a membership of more than 30 million. One of the most powerful interest groups in the nation, the AARP has thus far been able to defeat efforts to reduce spending for health care and social security.

The rise of the elderly will force the political system to deal with a number of vital issues. Should the care and support of the elderly be the nation's major priority? Or, should education and the creation of jobs be given preference? To what extent should the national government be obligated to provide financial support and health care to those elderly Americans who are wealthy? Is the public interest better served by a national budget that gives priority to environmental protection and the education of the young, or one that is dominated by the care and support of the elderly?

The successful resolution of these issues will be enormously complicated by the changing racial composition of American society. The prospect of an elderly population on the one hand—largely white, well-organized, and financially and politically resourceful—arrayed against a younger, multiracial, and multicultural population on the other suggests the enhanced likelihood of sustained and potentially divisive political conflict. This conflict will go to the very heart of the struggle over the redistribution of power and authority in American society.

## ECONOMIC CHANGE

Racial and demographic change will place enormous strain on the political system. The challenges posed by these changes are further complicated by the basic restructuring of the national economy. The globalization of the economy, the shift from an industrial to an information processing and high tech economy, and the continuing challenges to America's economic position in the international area, will combine to significantly alter the nation's political fabric. There is increasing evidence that the economy of the future will produce a relatively small elite of highly paid professionals and managers, and a very large group of marginally rewarded sales clerks, secretaries, fast-food workers, and janitors. The former group will reap enormous rewards from the system. The latter group will suffer underemployment, minimal job security, low wages, limited benefits, and little opportunity for advancement.[1]

Fast-food workers are typically at the low end of the wage scale. (Credit: Steve & Mary Skjold/© The Image Works)

For example, a huge number of the new jobs currently being created in the country pay no more than $5 to $9 an hour. Discount retailers such as Wal-Mart, Kmart, Target, and Home Depot are a major source of such jobs. In fact, the 500,000 jobs Wal-Mart provides ranks it as the nation's second-largest employer, trailing only General Motors. The pay offered by such jobs is unable to sustain a large middle class. Most employees of these discount chains earn minimum wages, while even assistant store managers are paid only $23,000 to $25,000 per year.

The implications of this trend toward low-paying jobs—typically, clerical employees earn only 40 percent of the wages received by manufacturing workers—are compounded by another disturbing development in the national economy. The *Presidential Commission on the Future of Worker-Management Relations* recently reported that the hourly pay of American workers, controlling for inflation, stagnated during the past 20 years and actually dropped for male workers. The Commission concluded that this development was "unprecedented in the past 75 years in this country."

Menial jobs, declining wages, and stagnating incomes do not bode well for the future of the American dream. Compounding this development is another, perhaps even more significant consequence of economic change. The gap between the rich and the poor today is the widest since the Census Bureau began maintaining such statistics in 1947. The poorest fifth of the American population receives only 4.4 percent of the nation's income. The richest fifth gets 45 percent. The rich are getting richer, and the gap between the haves and the have-nots is growing. Income inequality also cuts across racial lines. The top 5 percent of black families receive 47 percent of total black income.[2]

---

[1] Gary Burtless, (Ed.), *A Future of Lousy Jobs: The Changing Structure of U.S. Wages* (Washington, DC: Brookings Institution, 1990).
[2] Kevin Phillips, *The Politics of Rich and Poor* (New York: Random House, 1990).

Economic change in the United States has always caused profound political change. The transformation of the national economy from an agricultural to an industrial base in the late nineteenth and early twentieth centuries radically altered social and political relationships. Great cities developed as people moved from rural to urban-industrial areas. The ethnic and religious composition of the country changed as a result of a massive influx of immigrants from eastern and southern Europe. Political power was redistributed as labor unions began to organize, the middle class grew, and blacks immigrated from the South to midwestern and northeastern cities. This economic transformation also caused broad movements of political protest, beginning with the Populists and Progressives. The size and scope of government dramatically expanded as more programs and services were required by an increasingly complex society. The power and role of the bureaucracy grew as government at all levels assumed responsibility for regulating a wide array of social and economic activities. The prodigious industrial capacity and awesome technological prowess of the nation helped propel the American people to the very center of the world stage.

We can anticipate that the current economic transformation will also exert major impacts on the political and social fabric of the nation. It is likely that the middle class will continue to shrink. The great array of well-paying manufacturing jobs that sustained a robust middle class during the era of industrialization has been drastically curtailed. Huge numbers of blue-collar jobs in areas ranging from the production of automobiles and steel to apparel and appliances have been eliminated by foreign labor, computerization, and industrial robots. One possible consequence of a declining middle class is the enhanced likelihood of class conflict between the haves and the have-nots. The implications for the future stability of American democracy are significant.

Economic change will also affect interest groups and political parties. In 1953, 36 percent of the workforce claimed membership in labor unions. Today, only 12 percent does. Labor unions that represent manufacturing workers such as the AFL-CIO (American Federation of Labor-Congress of Industrial Organizations) and the UAW (United Auto Workers) once wielded enormous political influence. Times have changed. Public school teachers organized into entities such as the American Federation of Teachers are now the strongest arm of organized labor. In 1974, almost 2 million workers were idled in 424 strikes. In 1994, there were only 45 strikes idling only 322,000 workers. Economic change has also impacted on the Democratic Party. Once heavily dependent upon labor unions to turn out the vote, the decline of the industrial/manufacturing sector has forced the Democrats to seek out a more viable electoral strategy.

Economic change has also influenced the development of urban areas. Huge numbers of blue-collar, manufacturing jobs have been lost in the nation's inner cities in recent decades. The loss of these jobs has devastated countless central city neighborhoods, sapping their economic vitality and reducing the inhabitants to perpetual dependence on menial employment and welfare. The North Lawndale area of Chicago is typical of these neighborhoods. It has one bank, one supermarket, 48 state lottery agents, and 99 licensed bars and liquor stores. Six out of ten men and women who live there are unemployed. Between 1960 and 1970, North Lawndale lost three-fourths of its businesses and 25 percent of its jobs. During the next 10 years, 80 percent of the remaining manufacturing jobs were lost. Companies that moved out included Sears, International Harvester, Sunbeam, and Western Electric.[3]

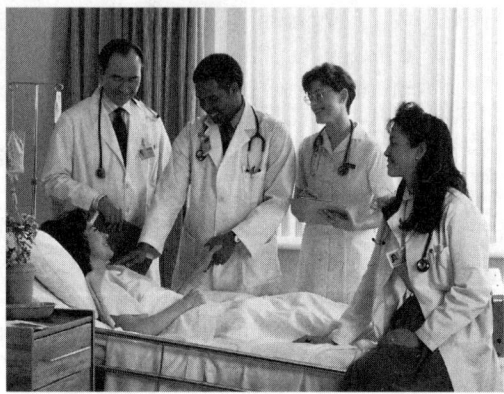

Well-educated professionals at work. (Credit: Jose L. Pelaez/The Stock Market)

Ironically, these same central cities have gained hundreds of thousands of new managerial, professional, and technical jobs. The difference is that these positions place a premium on education and specialized training.

Changes in the national economy have eroded the middle class, severely reduced the influence of labor unions, forced the Democratic Party to seek out new electoral strategies and coalitions, devastated central city neighborhoods, caused stagnating incomes for many and declining incomes for others, promoted a level of income inequality hitherto unknown, and placed a premium on advanced education as a precondition of individual success in the economic marketplace. These changes will likely exacerbate class conflict and racial animosity. They will also force Americans to eventually make increasingly difficult choices: What level of income inequality will be tolerated? Should the care and support of the elderly be given priority over the education of the young, particularly since education is so essential to success in the new economic era? Should education become a fundamental right guaranteed every American citizen, as vital and basic as more traditional constitutional rights? Is social security for the aged more in the "national interest" than job creation? How should the new wealth generated by a changing economy be distributed among the population?

## A NATION OF SUBURBS

In 1950, only a quarter of the population lived in the suburbs. By 1960, the suburban share of the population had risen to one-third. Today, half of all

---

[3] Jonathan Kozol, *Savage Inequalities* (New York: Crown, 1991).

Americans are suburbanites. When John Kennedy was elected president in 1960, the nation was a third urban, a third rural, and a third suburban. Today, the urban population has declined to 30 percent, and only one out of every 5 Americans lives in a rural area.

"White flight" from the central city to the suburbs represents more than a preference for private space and a life-style choice. Suburbanization is also proving to have enormous political consequences. First, suburbs tend to be heavily white, while central cities are dominated by nonwhites. As a result, the nation's population is intensely segregated along racial lines. Nationally, two-thirds of black students attend predominantly minority schools. In the inner cities, 15 out of every 16 black and Hispanic students are enrolled in schools with few whites. The northeast now has the most segregated schools in the country.

On a winter day in 1960, David Richmond, a frail black youth wearing a trench coat, made history when he and three other college students challenged the color barrier by taking seats at a F. W. Woolworth lunch counter in Greensboro, North Carolina. Their sit-in set off a national protest against segregation. Today, integration of public facilities is the law of the land. In many respects, however, integration is a dead issue. White flight to the suburbs has ensured that.

Another political impact of suburbanization is the privatization of American government. Although heavily Republican, it would be wrong to characterize suburban residents as antigovernment. They are not opposed to government spending. In fact, suburban governments spend vast and growing sums each year on schools, streets, parks, police, and fire protection. Suburbanites are strongly supportive of public spending that benefits their own community exclusively, and deeply resentful of a national government that takes their tax dollars for programs that they perceive as benefitting others.

Central cities are dominated by nonwhites. (Credit: David Jennings)

In the American system, people, jobs, and capital are essentially free to travel unimpeded across jurisdictional and political boundaries. A citizen or business dissatisfied with the mix of public and private goods and services available in one area is free—if they can afford the price of admission—to move to another. For example, the white family angered by poor schools, high crime, and the influx of racial minorities into their city neighborhood can vote with their feet. A much more decisive and effective participatory act than the vote, the widespread use of the "exit" option has transformed the social and political face of the nation. Local governments are in constant competition with one another employing both incentives ("quality" schools, a homogeneous population, low crime rates) and barriers (zoning ordinances, deed restrictions, expensive housing) to attract desirable consumers (middle- and upper-class whites) and exclude the undesirable (low-income, racial minorities).

Suburban government is private and exclusionary government. The suburbanization of the American population has caused further fragmentation and decentralization of political power and authority in the nation. Suburban government is a powerful alternative for those citizens who perceive that national and city governments are no longer responsive to their needs. Many believe that the national government pursues redistributive policies—policies that take from the haves in society and give to the have-nots. Wealth and opportunity are transferred from the better-off to the poor. The better-off perceive that they bear a disproportionate share of the costs of government programs and get little in return. According to this perspective, the national government is unresponsive, uncontrollable, and unaccountable.

Suburban governments, on the other hand, are both responsive and accountable. Residents of these jurisdictions do not want government to provide welfare or health care. They want government to protect their families and property. They want government to provide good schools, good police and fire protection, good parks, streets, drainage, garbage collection, and sanitation. They are willing to pay high taxes for these things if their tax dollars are spent exclusively for community residents. They want government to rigorously enforce zoning ordinances and deed restrictions in order to exclude undesirables and maintain property values.

The multiplicity of suburban governments in the nation encourages narrow, self-interested solutions to public problems. In a system where power is fragmented, the incentive is for the citizen to move away from his or her problems rather than to cooperate with others in an effort to solve them. Suburban governments are forced into competition with each other in an effort to attract preferred customers. Just as there is little incentive for citizens to cooperate, there is little incentive for governments to cooperate. Suburbanization—and the consequent fragmentation of political power into a multiplicity of competing governmental jurisdictions—leads to political isolation. Solutions to national problems such as crime and education become localized. Rather than engaging in broad-based, collective action on a national scale, suburban government encourages the opposite approach. Hire more police officers to patrol jurisdictional boundaries. Take steps to exclude from the neighborhood those persons perceived to be likely to commit crimes. Raise taxes, build better schools, hire more teachers. Political problem solving becomes particularized and self-contained. The confining of both responsibility and benefits to narrow jurisdictional boundaries leads to the further separation and isolation of communities that differ on the basis of race and class.

## THE CONFLICT OVER VALUES

Between 1890 and 1914, 16 million immigrants entered the country: Sicilians, Italians, Bulgarians, Poles, Greeks, Russian Jews, Czechs, Yugoslavians. Emma Lazarus, an American poet, wrote a sonnet about them. Her words—immortalized on the Statue of Liberty—are words of hope and welcome to the "huddled masses yearning to breathe free." Less memorable, but perhaps more prophetic, are the words written during the same period by Thomas Bailey Aldrich, editor of the *Atlantic Monthly*. He titled his poem "The Unguarded Gate":

> Wide open and unguarded stand our gates,
> And through them presses a wild motley throng—
> Men from the Volga and Tartar steppes,
> Featureless figures of the Hoang-Ho
> Malayan, Scythian, and Slav,
> These bringing with them unknown gods and rites,
> Those, tiger passions, here to stretch their claws,
> Accents of menace alien to our air,
> Voices that once the Tower of Babel knew!

When the eighteenth-century Frenchman Hector St. John de Crevecoeur asked the question, "What then is the American, this new man?" he already knew the answer. "Here individuals of all nations," he wrote, "are melted into a new race of men." The twentieth-century historian Arthur Schlesinger could write that the United States "escaped the divisiveness of a multiethnic society by a brilliant solution: the creation of a brand-new national identity. The point of America was not to preserve old cultures, but to forge a new, American culture."

Increasingly, the assumptions upon which both sets of these observations are based are in considerable doubt. The notion of America as a "melting pot" has long been discredited. And even the idea of a common "national identity" now invites controversy and dispute. Instead of a consensus with respect to the mix of cultural, ethnic, and ideological ingredients that comprise the "national identity," an often rancorous debate rages over whose America it is, and over who will take credit—and blame—for it. In significant degree, this debate centers on the issue of race.

Its supporters call it "multiculturalism"; its detractors derisively refer to it in more ominous terms—"political correctness." Whatever the label, the debate is about who will control the definition of what it means to be an American. The conflict revolves around the meaning of the nation's past, and the content of the national future. When Thomas Aldrich sounded the alarm over America's "unguarded gates," he gave voice to a deep-seated concern that the Anglo national heritage and culture would be overwhelmed by a swelling tide of immigrants bearing alien behaviors, religions, traditions, and languages. But for all their strangeness, those newcomers exhibited two traits that greatly eased their assimilation into the prevailing national identity. First, they were white. Second, they eagerly accepted the civic culture and ideology, even as many sought to maintain a considerable degree of ethnic separateness.

Today, the civic and political culture is under attack by a variety of non-white groups who question the accuracy and validity of a national history and heritage based almost exclusively on a Western European perspective. These groups insist that a major revision of the historical record is essential in order to acknowledge the vital contributions of non-Anglo races to the American experience. Instead of Columbus' "discovery" of America, they believe that the history books should reflect that he was "greeted" and "welcomed" by the millions of Native Americans who already inhabited the hemisphere. Rather than celebrating the Alamo as a heroic defense of liberty in the face of overwhelming odds, it should be seen as simply another incident in the onslaught of American imperialism. Instead of immortalizing the settling of the western frontier in terms of Anglo courage, sacrifice, and determination, it should be viewed as a war of greed and conquest, one that systematically destroyed countless Native American people and cultures.

These conflicts are about more than differing perspectives on the appropriate interpretation of the historical record. As America becomes an increasingly multicultural and multiracial society, intensified political conflict between different cultures and races can be expected. Already, bitter political struggles grounded in these racial and cultural confrontations dominate much of the public agenda. They include affirmative action, welfare reform, the content of the public school curriculum, immigration policy, English as the official language, crime, illegitimacy, poverty, and family values.

## CRIME, VIOLENCE, AND RACE

The typical police officer has to deal with more than eleven times as many violent crimes as the same police officer in the 1960s. Currently, there are 554,000 officers serving on state and local police forces. To achieve the same ratio of police officers to violent crimes in 1995 that existed in the 1960s, the nation would have to hire another 5 million police officers! The following statistics demonstrate the immensity of the problem:

- In 1960, 6 murders, 4 rapes, and 16 robberies were reported in New Haven, Connecticut. In 1990—with a population 14 percent smaller—New Haven reported 31 murders, 168 rapes, and 1,784 robberies.
- Every year for more than a decade, New York City has had almost 2,000 murders.
- The U.S. Justice Department estimates that 83 percent of all Americans will be victims of violent crime at least once in their lives. Almost 25 percent will be victims of three or more violent crimes.
- The overall imprisonment rate for black men, ages 25 to 29, is 7,200 per 100,000; for ages 30 to 34 it is 6,300 per 100,000. A study of black men, ages 18 to 34, in the District of Columbia found that on any day in 1991, 15 percent of these black males were in prison, 21 percent were on probation or parole, and another 6 percent were either awaiting trial or were being sought by the police.
- According to the U.S. Justice Department, one out of every 21 black males in this country will be murdered. This death rate is double that of American soldiers in World War II.
- The rate of murder committed by whites was 5.2 per 100,000 population, while it was 44.7 per 100,000 for blacks—a rate more than eight times higher than whites.
- In the past 10 years, 200,000 Americans have been murdered by fellow Americans. During a similar time period in Vietnam, 58,000 Americans were killed.

Senator Daniel Patrick Moynihan, Democrat from New York, has observed that the next 30 years are "already spoken for." What does he mean? In 1965, then-Professor Moynihan, a sociologist at Harvard University, published a study in which he concluded that the illegitimacy rate among blacks had grown to alarming proportions. He warned that one likely consequence of this development would be social disorder and violence. The Moynihan Report generated a storm of controversy. Many accused him of being a racist. Others argued that he was simply wrong. Still others attacked him for doing a disservice to the black community by providing intellectual justification for racist beliefs. The resulting furor created an atmosphere that made informed debate and discussion of the issue impossible. The implications of Moynihan's predictions were ignored.[4]

---

[4] Daniel P. Moynihan, *Family and Nation* (San Diego: Harcourt Brace Jovanovich, 1986).

Many scholars now believe that the high incidence of illegitimacy among blacks—in conjunction and interaction with drugs and the "pathology" of the ghetto—is a major factor fueling the disorder and violence among the urban underclass. Two out of every three blacks born in this country are born to single mothers. A growing proportion are being reared by neither parent. Although the number of young adults (the most crime-prone segment of the population) actually declined as a proportion of the population between 1985 and the present, the number of murders committed by ghetto youths dramatically increased. Professor James Fox of Northeastern University in Boston found that the homicide rate for blacks, ages 18 to 24, increased by 65 percent in just eight years, while the murder rate for young blacks, ages 14 to 17, more than doubled.

By the year 2000, the young blacks born in 1985 will turn 15. Three-fifths of them were born to single mothers. Professor John DeIulio of Princeton University concludes that the number of murders committed each year may well rise as high as 35,000 to 40,000, with the number of other violent crimes (robbery, rape, aggravated assault) rising at a similar rate.

The public fear generated by these developments has had—and will continue to have—a major impact upon the American political system.

### Political Impacts of Crime and Violence

The fear of crime has been a major factor in the exodus of whites to homogeneous suburban enclaves. The exit of middle-class blacks has been similarly affected. Professor Julius Wilson of the University of Chicago argues that this latter development has further devastated the ghetto by eliminating key role models for the urban underclass.[5]

The national epidemic of violence has also contributed to the shift in the public agenda over the past few decades from a concern with social justice to an emphasis on law and order. It has fueled the growing conservatism of the country. The rampant violence, disorder, and poverty that characterizes the urban underclass has been used by critics to attack federal programs such as welfare and public housing. Much of the current policy debate in the nation is dominated by problems and issues directly associated with the urban underclass—crime, welfare, the ineffectiveness of government programs, affirmative action, and the role of the federal government in addressing the problems of the poor and disadvantaged.

The rise of the "religious right" in American politics can also be attributed, in part, to a widespread reaction against illegitimacy, crime, drug use, lack of regard for authority, welfare dependency—and the government's costly and apparently ineffective efforts to combat these problems. The current

---

[5] William Julius Wilson, *The Truly Disadvantaged* (Chicago: University of Chicago Press, 1987).

Police officers making an arrest. (Credit: Jim Mahoney/The Image Works)

debate over "family values" stems in significant degree from this same general phenomenon.

The "pathology" of the ghetto—violence, drugs, female-headed families, poverty, joblessness, lack of opportunity—has operated to further isolate and alienate the urban underclass from the larger society. The potential explosiveness of such an environment—as evidenced by the Rodney King riots in Los Angeles—does not bode well for the future political stability of the nation.

The problems of the ghetto have also contributed to increasing the level of racial animosity and divisiveness in the country. Although a majority of black criminals commit their acts of violence against other blacks, it is also the case that a significant number of their victims are white.[6] Further, members of the black underclass account for a disproportionate share (in comparison to their percentage of the total population) of the violent crime in society. As significant perhaps as the reality of the situation is the *perception*. Many whites fear, and are angered by, what they perceive to be the rampant violence and social chaos and decay of the urban underclass.[7] Whether their perceptions—in conjunction with their apparent refusal to commit a level of public resources adequate to begin addressing the problem—define them as racists is one issue. It is more certain that these perceptions will continue to influence the course of policy and politics in the nation. Crime, race, and racism are significant factors in the political equation, and will likely impact how the electorate chooses, how public officials decide, how parties and interest groups react, and how the public agenda is constituted.

---

[6] Andrew Hacker, *Two Nations* (New York: Scribners, 1992).
[7] Thomas Edsall and Mary D. Edsall, *Chain Reaction: The Impact of Race, Rights, and Taxes on American Politics* (New York: Norton, 1991).

## Two Nations: Black and White

It would be foolhardy to discount the significance of race in the American political system. The importance of the issue is demonstrated by the following differences between blacks and whites:

- One out of every two black children lives below the poverty level. Only one out of seven white children lives below the poverty level.
- The net worth of the average white family is ten times that of the average black family.
- The illegitimacy rate of blacks is four times higher than the rate for whites.
- Among blacks under the age of 20, the murder rate is ten times higher than the murder rate among whites.
- More than a third of all black Americans live in only 16 metropolitan areas.[8] Most of them live in ghettos. No other group of Americans—including Hispanics—approaches this degree of residential segregation and social isolation.

American society is characterized by glaring inequalities of wealth, status, opportunity, privilege, and power. Some would even claim that it is essentially two separate countries. One of these societies is wealthy, sophisticated, and well-educated. Its citizens enjoy the benefits of a prosperous economy, vast personal freedoms, and a government that is both efficient and responsive. Opportunity abounds, crime rates are low, and individuals are secure in their person and property. The other society has little in common with the first. It is an alien environment of ghettos, institutionalized poverty, drugs, violence, crime, police brutality, racial discrimination, teenage pregnancies, fatherless households, welfare checks and food stamps, inadequate health care, inferior schools, high unemployment, and child and wife abuse.[9] The problems are so severe and the prospects for improvement so dim that many despair that things will ever get better. This is the dark underside of American politics. We can anticipate the eventual likelihood of heightened racial conflict as a result.

## THE DECLINE OF THE NATIONAL GOVERNMENT

The "high tide" of national power has passed. The shift in political power to state and local governments—the reversal of a trend toward an increasingly powerful national government that began with the Civil War—represents a significant development within the American political system. The reasons for this shift of power and responsibility within the federal framework include:

---

[8] Douglas Massey and Nancy Denton, *American Apartheid: Segregation and the Making of the Underclass* (Cambridge, MA: Harvard University Press, 1993).
[9] Christopher Jencks and Paul E. Peterson, Eds., *The Urban Underclass* (Washington, DC: Brookings Institution, 1991).

- The national government is broke. If it were a corporation—or family for that matter—it would have long since been forced to file for protection from its creditors under bankruptcy laws. It is so deeply in debt that interest payments alone account for $14 of every $100 it spends. Although budget expenditures are certainly not the only measure of governmental effectiveness and power, the absence of money has dramatically curtailed the aggressiveness with which the national government once pursued a variety of programs, services, and policies.
- The decline of the national security state has also had an impact. The United States has not fought a major war in a quarter of a century. Prior to that time it fought four major conflicts—World War I, World War II, Korea, Vietnam—and dozens of lesser ones in only fifty years. These wars, in conjunction with the military/security apparatus required by the confrontation between the "Cold War" superpowers, provided the rationale for—and conferred legitimacy upon—the continued expansion of national power. With the end of the Cold War, however, the government can no longer employ national security interests to justify increasing levels of expenditures in areas such as foreign aid, education, space exploration, and research and development.

Another factor that accounts for the decline of national power is the growing belief on the part of many that certain problems are simply not susceptible to solution through the efforts and expenditures of the national government. Some argue that well-intended federal programs (welfare, for example) have actually made things worse. The growing conservatism in the nation is fueled in significant degree by widespread disenchantment with—and even antipathy toward—the national government. The criticisms of "big government" include high taxes, runaway spending, unbalanced budgets, excessive regulation, bureaucratic waste and inefficiency, and support of controversial programs such as welfare, affirmative action, and other civil rights programs.

Economic and demographic change has seriously weakened the core constituencies that the Democratic Party—the most forceful institutional advocate of an aggressive national government—has traditionally relied upon. As discussed earlier, the decline of a manufacturing-based economy has eroded the strength and influence of labor unions. In addition, the loss of another traditional constituency—the once "solid South"—and the declining significance of yet another (big city interests), have operated to further weaken the Democrats. As a result, their efforts to expand national power and champion the interests of the poor, the working class, and racial minorities have suffered severe setbacks.

## The Federal System and Change

The precise contours of the emerging federal system cannot yet be perceived. However, we can suggest several factors that are likely to give it identifiable shape. First, the states will be forced to assume a greater share of the burden of governing as the national government continues to shed both financial and functional responsibility for programs and services. Second, suburban and other local governments will continue to grow in power and importance. This decentralization of political authority in the nation will enhance the likelihood of several long-run developments. For example, states—and particularly suburban governments—will exhibit little enthusiasm for the variety of costly social welfare programs that the national government has traditionally provided. In addition, states and localities will be limited in their assumption of new program responsibilities by the need to balance their budgets. Further, state and local governments have typically relied upon regressive taxes (those that impose a heavier tax burden on lower-income families) such as sales and property taxes to generate revenues. Consequently, the growing revenue needs of these governments will, in the long-run, translate into a further redistribution of the tax burden between the rich and poor.

Finally, it is probable that the gradual shift of political power and responsibility from the national government to the states will be accompanied by an equally steady shift in the focus and purpose of government. Unlike the national government, the states will be less inclined to champion the interests of consumers, minorities, the disadvantaged, and the needy. They will be more likely to emphasize basic services and functions such as transportation, police protection, education, and the criminal justice system.

But the shift in political power from the national government to states and localities will entail more than a systematic bias against higher taxes and social welfare programs. It will also initiate an era of more exclusive government. As discussed earlier, suburban jurisdictions are inclined to pursue narrow, self-interested solutions to policy problems. With the decline of national authority and responsibility, the danger exists that efforts at shaping national solutions to problems that afflict the country as a whole will be abandoned in favor of more parochial approaches. Local and regional interests—rather than the national interest—will be more likely to prevail.

## CONCLUSION

Several powerful trends in American society will influence—and be influenced by—the political system. We have identified and briefly discussed these developments. Politics is the conflict over scarce resources. That conflict will be shaped and exacerbated in the coming decades by a shifting panorama of new and powerful groups. The public pie will be resliced by the array of new interests emerging from the process of change discussed above. Hispanics, Asian-Americans, the elderly, the new economic elite ("symbolic analysts" in Robert Reich's terminology), religious fundamentalists, and suburban residents—among others—will increasingly define and interpret the political rules and dominate the public agenda.

The political conflicts generated by these changes will be expressed and resolved through the vote, the laws passed by Congress, and judicial decisions. However, they will also be expressed through population shifts, and in decisions on the part of individual citizens as to where they choose to live. They will be manifested in terms of the level of racial animosity and class conflict, and in the way in which wealth and opportunity are distributed among the population. As American society becomes older, browner, and more unequal, public officials will be subjected to enormous strains and pressures. They will be forced to deal with the nation's economic base; the decline of a once vast and robust middle class; the apparently intractable problems of racial hatred, crime, and drugs; the decay of the nation's once mighty cities and the corresponding drain of power and resources to segregated suburbs; the increasingly multicultural and multiracial nature of American society; and the widening gaps among Americans with respect to opportunity, income, and wealth.

The political system does not have the option of deferring action in response to these problems. A multiracial and multicultural society will produce enormous political strains and tensions. The country has had past experience with demographic change. But the great waves of ethnic migration in the nineteenth and the first part of the twentieth century were different in one fundamental respect: The new arrivals were white.

We can already see indications of the tension these demographic transformations are likely to produce. One ominous sign is a rise in the level of racial bitterness and instances of racially motivated violence and brutality. In the classroom, there are conflicts over bilingual education and multicultural curriculum. Black grievances and discontent may increase if they perceive that the increased political and economic power enjoyed by Hispanics and Asians has been obtained at their expense. One potential interracial conflict will incorporate an element of intergenerational tension as well. As the white population ages, an increasing number of retirees will place heavy demands upon the social security system. Ironically, these largely white retirees will be supported by a heavily nonwhite working population. The heightened racial and class conflict generated by these changes will be further complicated by economic discontent and the growing income gap between the rich and poor.

## RECOMMENDED READINGS

Auletta, Ken. 1982. *The Underclass.* New York: Random House.
Burtless, Gary, Ed. 1990. *A Future of Lousy Jobs: The Changing Structure of U.S. Wages.* Washington, DC: Brookings Institution.

Duncan, Greg J. 1984. *Years of Poverty, Years of Plenty: The Changing Economic Fortunes of America's Workers and Families.* Ann Arbor, MI: Survey Research Center.

Edsall, Thomas. 1984. *The New Politics of Inequality.* New York: Norton.

Edsall, Thomas, and Mary D. Edsall. 1991. *Chain Reaction: The Impact of Race, Rights, and Taxes on American Politics.* New York: Norton.

Ellwood, David T. 1988. *Poor Support: Poverty in the American Family.* New York: Basic Books.

Jencks, Christopher, and Paul E. Peterson, Eds. 1991. *The Urban Underclass.* Washington, DC: Brookings Institution.

Katz, Michael B. 1986. *In the Shadow of the Poorhouse: A Social History of Welfare in America.* New York: Basic Books.

Moynihan, Daniel P. 1986. *Family and Nation.* San Diego: Harcourt Brace Jovanovich.

Phillips, Kevin. 1990. *The Politics of Rich and Poor.* New York: Random House.

Phillips, Kevin. 1994. *Boiling Point.* New York: Random House.

Wilson, William Julius. 1987. *The Truly Disadvantaged.* Chicago: University of Chicago Press.

U.S. Bureau of the Census. 1995. *Historical Statistics of the United States: Colonial Times to 1970.* Washington, DC: U.S. Government Printing Office.

# 2

# The Political Origins of the American Republic

Accumulated Evils
   *The Common Herd*
   *Network of Dependencies*
   *The Liberation of the Common Man*
   *Mass Participation*

Equality
   *Classical Republicanism*
   *The Common Man and Republicanism*
   *Aristocracy of Talent*
   *Popular Government*

Economics and Politics
   *Daniel Shays*
   *The Rebellion*
   *Alexander Hamilton*

State Legislatures
   *Radical Democracy*
   *Radical Laws*

Direct Democracy

Elite Fears

---

By the malign influence of the moon's eclipses, the United States of America will be troubled with . . . domestic quarrels, and contentions of every kind.
—Samuel Ellsworth, Astronomer, 1786

The proposition that (the people) are the best keeper of their liberties is not true. They are the worst conceivable, they are no keepers at all. They can neither act, judge, think, or will.
—John Adams, 1787

## ACCUMULATED EVILS

The decade of the 1780s was a time of deep disillusionment for many of the leaders of the revolutionary era. In a commencement address at Harvard College in July 1787, one graduate spoke of the country "groaning under the intolerable burden of accumulated evils." Another observed that "mankind are not made to govern themselves." To another it seemed as if "the people were as capable of despotism as any prince." Even George Washington wrote, "We have, probably, had too good an opinion of human nature in forming our confederation." Many spoke out against the "blustering, haughty, licentious, self-seeking men" who were gaining the "ear of the people."[1] What could have happened to cause John Adams to describe the people as incapable of thinking, acting, and judging? What had happened to the optimism of the revolutionary years?

It was, in large part, a question of expectations. What had the leaders expected of the revolution? What had common men expected? To answer these questions, we need to examine the political and social fabric of colonial America, and evaluate the impact of the Revolution upon political and social arrangements. We will then be in a better position to understand how patterns of political authority were transformed by the Revolution. Further, we will see how the new Constitution was shaped and fashioned in response to the profound changes initiated by this transformation.

## The Common Herd

In colonial America, before the Revolution, there was a clear distinction between gentlemen and commoners, with the former holding the latter in contempt. Alexander Hamilton wrote about "the unthinking populace," George Washington referred to farmers as "the grasying multitude," Governor Morris thought the people had "no morals but their interests," and John Adams described them as the "common herd of mankind." The masses were frequently described in the most derogatory of terms: ignorant, vulgar, idiotic, selfish, narrow-minded, superstitious, and bigoted. They were an "unthinking mob," enveloped in a "mist of ignorance." One scholar estimates that this powerful distinction between elites and masses was recognized in all of the colonies, with approximately one in twenty-five adult white males accorded the status of gentleman in the southern colonies, and one in ten enjoying that title in the northern ones.[2]

The lowly status of many Americans was recognized in law as well as in social perception and economic standing. For example, it has been estimated that from one-half to two-thirds of the immigrants to the colonies before the Revolution arrived as indentured servants. Having traded five to seven years of their labor in return for passage to the colonies from Europe, they could be driven to market "like cattle . . . and exposed to sale in public fairs as so many brute beasts." The legal status of indentured servants was similar to that of slaves. Labor was scarce in the colonies and they were valuable economic commodities. As such, they had to obtain their owner's permission before they could hold or sell property, marry, or even leave the premises. They could be sold, rented out, seized by a creditor for nonpayment of debts, and disposed of

---

[1] Quoted in Gordon S. Wood, *The Radicalism of the American Revolution* (New York: Knopf, 1992).
[2] *Ibid.*

in their master's will. Their terms of indenture were carefully regulated by legal contracts. Even native-born children could be "bound out" by their parents. Foreign visitors were struck by the harshness of the system, and were frequently unable to distinguish between the treatment of white indentured servants and that of black slaves.

## Network of Dependencies

The system of indentured labor was only one aspect of the stratified and hierarchal nature of colonial America. Other more subtle but equally powerful arrangements contributed to a complex network of dependencies and obligations. The mechanism of credit, for example, bound the lower classes to the elite. In an age when the ordinary citizen had no access to banks, credit unions, mortgage companies, savings and loans associations, and credit cards, a wealthy patron was frequently the only available source of credit. A network of dependencies was created as a result. In turn, the lending of money provided a major source of income for the wealthy. Freed from the need to work for a living, many gentlemen relied upon their income from interest on loans to achieve both financial independence as well as a considerable degree of influence in community affairs.

Wealth also separated the classes. The Penns, the Calverts in Maryland, and Lord Fairfax in Virginia owned huge estates of several million acres. A powerful landholding aristocracy developed along the Hudson Valley in New York and among the plantation owners in the southern colonies. Great wealth was also concentrated in the hands of merchants and lawyers in New York, Boston, Philadelphia, Newport, and Charleston. There is also evidence that the rich were getting richer. One study found that during the period 1687–1774, the wealthiest 5 percent increased its share of the wealth from 33 percent to 55 percent. Amazingly, the bottom half of the population in Boston and Philadelphia owned only 5 percent of the wealth. One out of every four adult males in Philadelphia was poor by the standards of the day.

Family and kinship were extremely important factors in colonial politics. In fact, political life was dominated by competition between opposing family networks. Important political groups were identified by family names—the DeLanceys in New York, the Ogdens in New Jersey, the Wentworths in New Hampshire. In colonial America, social status translated into political authority. Gentlemen from these wealthy families saw political office and responsibility as an obligation. Officeholding was perceived as a personal sacrifice, a duty to be discharged by virtue of membership in the social elite. Colonial politics, then, was dominated by considerations of class, social status, family, and friendship ties. The lower classes were dependent upon and obligated to the elite in a variety of ways—through indentured servitude, for credit, for assistance in obtaining employment and services. The personal reputation and social standing of a gentleman—rather than his political program or philosophy—were the measure employed to evaluate suitability for holding office. Particular political positions frequently remained in the same family, passed from generation to generation. The legitimacy of political authority flowed from social status and class rather then from the consent of the governed.

## The Liberation of the Common Man

The Revolution turned that world upside down. The war was waged to achieve independence from Britain. It also liberated the common man from a tradition of dependency, and introduced the powerful notion of egalitarianism into American political life.[3] The struggle against the British had the effect of causing ordinary American citizens to organize and press their political claims. Even before the war, citizen groups were demanding that British goods be boycotted. In 1772, the artisans and craftsmen of Philadelphia created an organization known as the Patriotic Society. It was the first nonreligious interest group in the history of the state. Similar groups formed in the other colonies, and soon they were running slates of candidates for various offices. In 1770, workers in Philadelphia were victorious in elections for four of ten city offices. The ordinary American had found a new political voice. As one of their number observed at the time, "If ever your rights are preserved, it must be through the virtue and integrity of the middling sort, as farmers, tradesmen . . . who best know the sweets of liberty." Politics was no longer the exclusive preserve of the elite, and they knew it. In 1775, the royal governor of Georgia described the committee running Savannah as consisting of "the lowest people, chiefly carpenters, shoemakers, blacksmiths, etc. with a Jew at their head." Another elite observer noted that "the many headed power of the people, who have hitherto been obediently made use of by their numbers . . . have discovered their own strength and importance, and are not now so easily governed by their former leaders."

## Mass Participation

Ordinary Americans took to heart Samuel Adams' admonition that the people had the right "to assemble upon all occasions to consult measures for promoting liberty and happiness." During the 1770s and throughout the war, average citizens actively participated in political affairs. Citizen committees, associations, and conventions performed a variety of political functions and duties including tax collection and the regulation of prices and wages. Citizen groups made decisions about the militia, regulated trade, monitored the activities of the courts, and appointed various military and political officials. During the War, these committees, associations, and conventions assumed responsibility

---

[3] Robert Middlekauff, *The Glorious Cause* (New York: Oxford University Press, 1982).

for dealing with economic issues on a regional and even interstate basis. At first, they were authorized to undertake these activities by their respective state legislatures or the Continental Congress. When the legislatures and Congress withdrew their support, however, they continued on their own.

## EQUALITY

A transformation in the political perceptions of ordinary American citizens took place during this period. They rejected the dependencies and restrictions that had regulated and limited their political behavior in prerevolutionary society. They were no longer willing to recognize and accept their "place" or station in life. Political authority was now grounded in the popular consent of the people, rather than anchored in class distinctions, status, and family connections. According to one scholar,

> Equality was . . . the most radical and most powerful ideological force let loose in the Revolution. Once invoked, the idea of equality could not be stopped, and it tore through American society and culture with awesome power . . . Within decades following the Declaration of Independence, the United States became the most egalitarian nation in the history of the world . . . Equality became so potent for Americans because it came to mean that everyone was really the same as everyone else, not just at birth, not in talent or property or wealth, and not just in some transcendental religious sense of the equality of all souls. Ordinary Americans came to believe that no one in a basic down-to-earth and day-in- and day-out manner was really better than anyone else. That was equality as no other nation has ever quite had it.[4] (p. 67)

The greater emphasis upon equality was reflected in legal changes as well. After the Revolution, the states altered their inheritance laws to ensure more equality among sons and daughters. Indentured servitude became a thing of the past. Divorce laws were liberalized, husbands no longer exercised virtually complete control over their wives, and women were given more power to acquire, hold, and dispose of property. Another development that severely weakened the prerevolutionary political and social structure was the emigration of the Loyalists. It is estimated that as many as 500,000 Americans remained loyal to the British—a number that accounted for one out of every five white Americans. Perhaps 80,000 of them departed the country during the War. Significantly, many of them had exercised enormous political and economic influence before the War. They counted among their number some of the most powerful merchants and landowners in the country. Their departure radically altered a

---

[4] Wood, *The Radicalism of the American Revolution*.

political and social structure that had been primarily based upon the claims of class, wealth, patronage, and kinship connections.

## Classical Republicanism

Ordinary Americans took to heart John Adams' pronouncement that there are only two classes of men: freemen and slaves. They believed the words of the Declaration of Independence, that all men are created equal. Why, then, the profound disillusionment of the revolutionary leaders with the developments of the 1780s? What had happened to transform optimism into pessimism? Why the low regard for the ability of the people to govern themselves? Why were the people now to be feared? To answer these questions, we first need to evaluate the dominant ideology of the revolutionary era: classical republicanism. According to one scholar,

> the colonial and Revolutionary ideal lay, not in the pursuit of private matters, but in the shared public life of civic duty, in the subordination of individual interests . . . Citizens were defined and fulfilled by participation in political community. To the first American generation the political community was a single organic whole, binding each of its members into a civic body of shared interests that transcended individual concerns . . . Here, then, is an image of a virtuous, united people, bound together by a shared public good, and active in civic affairs . . . Americans were no longer celebrants of self but participants in a shared public life.[5] (p. 32)

Gordon Wood writes that,

> According to classical republican tradition, man was by nature a political being, a citizen who achieved his greatest moral fulfillment by participating in a self-governing republic . . . Liberty was realized when the citizens were virtuous-that is, willing to sacrifice their private interest for the sake of the community, including serving in public office without pecuniary reward. To be completely virtuous citizens, men-never women, because it was assumed they were never independent-had to be free from dependence and from the petty interests of the marketplace. Any loss of independence and virtue was corruption . . . Public virtue was the sacrifice of private desires and interests for the public interest . . . All men of genius and leisure, all gentlemen, had an obligation to serve the state . . . Republicanism thus put an enormous burden on individuals. They were expected to suppress their private wants and interests . . . Precisely because republics required civic virtue among their citizens, they were very fragile polities, extremely liable to corruption. Republics demanded far more morally from their citizens than monarchies did of their subjects. In monarchies each man's desire to do what was right in his own eyes could be restrained by fear or force,

---

[5] James A. Morone, *The Democratic Wish* (New York: Basic Books, 1990).

by patronage or honor. In republics, however, each man must somehow be persuaded to sacrifice his personal desires, his luxuries, for the sake of the public good . . . In their purest form [Republics] had no adhesives, no bonds holding themselves together, except their citizens' voluntary patriotism and willingness to obey public authority. Without virtue and self-sacrifice republics would fall apart.[6] (p. 104)

## The Common Man and Republicanism

Significantly, however, the revolutionary leaders did not anticipate that ordinary citizens—men who toiled for a living—would run the government in this new and virtuous republic. They did not foresee that butchers and bakers and candlestick makers would actively participate in the important political decisions of the Republic. Although Thomas Jefferson believed that the independent farmer would be capable of "virtue," many felt that ordinary citizens were simply unable to subdue their narrow, private interests. They were certainly ill-equipped to hold high office. The republican idealists had no intention of turning control of government over to the common man. Although they had a higher regard for the people than was held in a monarchy, what they really had in mind was an "aristocracy of merit." An elite would still run things. The difference was that in a republic, "a man's merit [would] rest entirely with himself without any regard to family, blood, or connection." This "natural aristocracy," in Jefferson's words, would replace the old aristocracy based on birth, class, and wealth. No longer would men of talent and ambition be denied the realization of their full potential simply because of the accident of birth. That was one of the powerful meanings of the American Revolution.

## Aristocracy of Talent

In this "aristocracy of talent" even the highest political office would be open to men of merit and virtue, regardless of wealth or social standing. Although the ordinary citizen was poorly qualified to hold such office, his son—by dint of talent and hard work—might well aspire to that goal. Such ambition would require a liberal education, an enlightened character, and virtue—in short, the attributes of a gentleman. Remarkably, however, these attainments for the son of an ordinary, working man were possible in a republic. In fact, many of the revolutionary leaders—John Adams, Thomas Jefferson, John Jay, James Madison, John Marshall—were "first-generation gentlemen." Their fathers, unlike themselves, were not liberally educated and "enlightened." It is little wonder, then that these members of the "natural aristocracy,"—one based upon merit and talent—would expect their successors to possess traits and characteristics identical to their own. Ordinary men were unfit to participate directly in

---

[6] Wood, *The Radicalism of the American Revolution,* p. 104.

important political decisions because they lacked the enlightened attributes of a gentlemen. But there was another reason. The average citizen was simply too deeply involved in making a living, in "getting ahead," and in pursuing narrow, private, self-interest. Virtue and enlightenment were incapable of flourishing in such an environment.

## Popular Government

But something happened during the decades of the 1770s and 1780s that would set the Republic on a route the leaders had never envisioned. The people had gotten a taste of what it was like to participate directly in those political decisions that affected their lives. The Revolution had unleashed the force of egalitarianism, and now ordinary citizens were inclined to believe that they could organize into groups and press their private claims upon public authorities. According to this perspective, government existed not to advance an abstract public interest, but to assist citizens in attaining their concrete private interests. Further, ordinary citizens increasingly proclaimed that they were fully qualified to act as their own judges with respect to the appropriate ends of government. These views were deeply frightening to the republican idealists. If each citizen were as good as every other citizen, regardless of talent, education, or the enlightened nature of his character, then the "virtuous" man could lay no legitimate claim to exercising political power on behalf of the people. Instead, it logically followed that the people could act and decide on their own. As one artisan of the period observed, "If ever your rights are preserved, it must be through the virtue and integrity of the middling sort, as farmers, tradesmen . . . who best know the sweets of liberty." Another representative of a citizens' group wrote that "Every man who honestly supports a family by useful employment is honourable enough for any office in the state . . . all have an equal right to declare their interests, and to have them regarded."[7]

# ECONOMICS AND POLITICS

The years following the Revolutionary War were ones particularly well-suited to encouraging the articulation of interests and the generation of class conflicts. Hundreds of millions of dollars in paper currency had been issued to carry on the war effort. The requirements of the armies in the field on both sides had dramatically stimulated production and trade. With the end of the war, however, the military's demand for goods disappeared. The government stopped printing paper money. The small tradesmen, farmers, artisans, and craftsmen who had prospered during the war found themselves in serious economic trouble. The war effort had caused them to produce and spend. Now

---

[7] Quoted in Wood, *The Radicalism of the American Revolution*.

many were deeply in debt, and the market for their goods and services had vanished. These small farmers and businessmen wanted the government to issue more paper currency. They demanded that they be allowed to pay their debts and taxes in paper. Without a large supply of such money, their customers could not buy their goods and services. They, in turn, could not pay their debts, and their families could not improve their standard of living. However, wealthy merchants and the landed gentry had a different perspective on the paper currency issue. They were deeply suspicious of paper money. Its value was unknown or subject to erratic fluctuations. The more paper money issued, the less valuable it became. Consequently, wealthy merchants and landowners insisted that debts be paid in specie—gold and silver coin. They also demanded that the mortgages they held on small farms and businesses be repaid in specie. Unfortunately for the small farmer and businessman who owed these debts, there was very little specie in circulation, and almost no way to get one's hands on any. If the government refused to issue more paper money, and if creditors insisted upon payment in specie, then the outcome was inevitable: foreclosure and bankruptcy. The problem was particularly acute for those ordinary citizens who, as soldiers, had borne the brunt of the fighting during several years of hard war (the longest war in the nation's history until Vietnam), who had been absent from their farms and trades for years, and who had been paid for their military service in paper currency!

## Daniel Shays

The stage was now set for one of the most decisive political conflicts in American history. It was in the words of one historian "truly a critical period . . . perhaps the most critical moment in all the history of America." The significance of the political choices that had to be made, and the impact of those decisions upon the lives of ordinary citizens, can be illustrated by looking at the experiences of two very different Americans of the period. The first of these men was Daniel Shays.[8] Shays was born in western Massachusetts, received little in the way of a formal education, and grew up as a farm laborer. He worked hard, saved his money, and eventually purchased a small farm near the community of Pelham. Home to less than a thousand people, Pelham had 125 houses, 98 barns, two mills, three taverns, and a handful of stores. The farms in the area were small, with the average in 1760 being 6.4 tilled acres. This figure had dropped to 5.2 acres in 1771, and had further declined to only 2.3 acres in 1784. When the colonies declared their independence from Britain, Daniel Shays enlisted in the state militia and obtained a commission as an officer. Captain Shays was wounded at Bunker Hill during the battle and decorated for valor after it. His performance in other battles during the war was so striking

---

[8] Richard Severo and Lewis Milford, *The Wages of War* (New York: Simon & Schuster, 1989).

that none other than the Frenchman Marquis de Lafayette took notice of it. In fact, Lafayette bestowed an extraordinary honor on Shays by presenting him with an ornamental sword. Daniel Shays was known as a direct and down-to-earth man, and he showed it by promptly selling the sword awarded to him by the famous Frenchman. He used the proceeds to repay a debt. When his brother officers expressed their outrage, he informed them that he already had a sword and didn't need another. After the War, Shays returned to his farm and soon found himself deeply in debt, and in serious trouble with his creditors.

Shays' Rebellion. (The Granger Collection, New York)

The economic troubles experienced by small farmers in Massachusetts were similar to the problems facing farmers everywhere. The yeomen measured wealth in terms of crops and land. They depended heavily upon a barter system as the dominant means of exchange. Unfortunately, their mortgages and debts were held by men who demanded payment in gold and silver. The farmers of western Massachusetts could expect no help from state government. In fact, Governor James Bowdoin, as well as many members of the judiciary and state legislature, were heavily involved in currency and securities speculation. The economic difficulties facing the farmers were made even worse when the legislature decided to retire the state's war debt by imposing a direct tax on real estate. Since merchants had invested most of their wealth in goods rather than in real estate, they escaped the brunt of the tax burden. It was the farmers whose wealth was measured primarily in terms of land who were hardest hit. Further, they were required to pay these taxes in specie. Paper currency was unacceptable.

The results were predictable. Foreclosures on defaulted mortgages and confiscation of property for nonpayment of taxes rapidly mounted. The farmers petitioned the state legislature in Boston for debtor relief. They wanted to be able to pay their debts and taxes in paper currency, and demanded as well more time in which to pay them. Their requests were ignored. Farmers in both Massachusetts and surrounding states were hardhit. In the town of Worcester, 145 citizens were sent to debtor's prison. Seventy-three towns in Massachusetts sent petitions to the legislature requesting that it halt the confiscation of farms, that it issue paper currency, and that it put an end to the jailing of citizens for the nonpayment of taxes. In Connecticut, 500 farmers were thrown into prison in 1786 for nonpayment of taxes. Forty-one towns in New Hampshire petitioned the legislature in that state for debtor relief.

## The Rebellion

The desperate farmers in western Massachusetts had come to see their own government as the enemy. Most of them had fought for their country in the War for Independence against Britain, but this was not the kind of freedom they had bargained for. Finally, their anger and frustration initiated a series of events that would profoundly influence the future course of the new republic. In August 1786, 1,500 farmers under the leadership of Luke Day, a former officer in the Revolutionary Army, took matters into their own hands and took control of the debtor court in Northhampton. They called themselves "regulators." It was their intent to regulate the court, to prevent it from foreclosing on more farms. In the weeks to come, farmers seized control of debtor courts in a number of other towns as well. The protest spread into Connecticut and Vermont. Governor Bowdoin raised an army to put down the insurrection. Daniel Shays, now the reluctant leader of the rebellious farmers, led a ragtag army of his own. It was no contest. After a series of skirmishes and minor engagements, the rebellion collapsed. Daniel Shays went into exile. (He died in New York in 1825.)

The insurrection had not been much. But the reaction to it would prove to have enormous significance. Thomas Jefferson was almost alone in his assessment of it. In a letter to Abigail Adams, the wife of John Adams, written in February 1787, Jefferson wrote "The spirit of resistance to government is so valuable that I wish it to be always kept alive. I like a little rebellion now and then. It is like a storm in the atmosphere." In a prophetic letter to James Madison, Jefferson also wrote, "The late rebellion in Massachusetts has given more alarm than I think it should have done." In fact, Shays' little rebellion had deeply frightened many members of the elite. What concerned them even more than the violence was that the newly elected members of the state legislature in Boston were now more responsive to the needs and demands of the debtor class. The revolutionary leaders were already dismayed by the apparent corruption and rejection of republican values and principles among the masses of people. Now the people were seizing control of various state legislatures and adopting measures designed to provide debtor relief. To the masses it might look like democracy in action. To virtuous gentlemen of wealth, position, and power, however, it looked like a virtual assault on property and liberty.

## Alexander Hamilton

The life of Alexander Hamilton is illustrative of the enormously talented and extremely influential "first generation gentlemen" who dominated the political decisions of the era.⁹ It was a life whose origins were as inauspicious as those of Daniel Shays. But through genius and sheer diligence Hamilton was able to join the "aristocracy of talent," and along the way acquire the gentlemanly attributes of virtue, enlightened character, and a liberal education. At least that is the way Hamilton and other members of the elite would have described the experience.

He was born the illegitimate son of James Hamilton and Rachael Faucett Lavien in the West Indies where his father had

Alexander Hamilton. (Credit: Archive Photos)

gone to find his fortune. He did not find that, but he did find Rachael who at the time was inconveniently married to another man. According to her husband and other witnesses who testified against her in subsequent divorce proceedings, Rachael had given "herself up to whoring with everyone." In addition to the allegation of loose morals she was also accused of being "shameless, rude, and ungodly." James Hamilton lived with Rachael and Alexander until his son was eleven-years-old. He then abandoned them. Alexander's mother died when he was fourteen, and after her death, the boy went to work for a company whose business it was to trade West Indian sugar, molasses, and rum for American lumber, livestock, and agricultural produce. Hamilton quickly rose to the position of chief deputy to the owner. Already distinguished by a powerful intellect and deep ambition, he wrote a friend at the time that "my ambition is so prevalent, that I condemn the groveling condition of a clerk or the like, to which my Fortune Condemns me and would willingly risk my life to exalt my station. I wish there was a war."[10] The young Hamilton must have impressed his employer mightily, for the man sold two shiploads of sugar and designated the proceeds exclusively to financing Hamilton's education in America. Hamilton's adolescent experience vividly illustrates one of the few avenues of upward social mobility available to the low-born in the prerevolutionay period. Youngsters who did not enjoy the enormous advantages of wealth and kinship connections could little aspire to attain entry to the ranks of the gentleman class. Unless he had a patron—a powerful benefactor who would adopt

---

[9] Jacob E. Cooke, *Alexander Hamilton* (New York: Scribners, 1982).
[10] *Ibid.*

the particularly promising young man and carefully groom him by way of education and connections for a higher station in life.

After arriving in the colonies, Hamilton prepared for a year and then enrolled in King's College in New York City in 1773. His education was interrupted by the war he had hoped for. After being commissioned as a officer in the New York state militia he met another powerful patron and benefactor—General George Washington. The commanding general was impressed with the young officer and appointed him one of his aides de camp. He performed so well in this capacity that Washington assigned him a number of important administrative, diplomatic, and military tasks. In the role of a key aide to the commanding general of the Continental Army, Hamilton had the opportunity to meet and impress a large number of prominent and highly influential Americans. During the War, he also married into a wealthy and aristocratic family. Hamilton topped off this already splendid young career by heroically leading a bayonet assault in the final defeat of the British forces at Yorktown.

After the war, he studied law for three months and was admitted to the bar. He served in the Continental Congress, and in 1787 was elected as a delegate from New York to the Constitutional Convention. Hamilton had come a very long way in a very short period of time. Born illegitimate, abandoned by his father, and left homeless and penniless by the death of his mother, he had obtained a college education, served as a key aide to one of the most influential men in the country, married into a wealthy and socially prominent family, established himself in the legal profession, and became one of the most powerful officials in the new national government. President Washington appointed him to be the first Secretary of the Treasury. To many of the revolutionary leaders Hamilton epitomized how far a man of merit, virtue, and enlightened character could go in a new social order based on an "aristocracy of talent," rather than one founded on birth, blood, and inherited wealth.

Both Daniel Shays and Alexander Hamilton were of lowly origin. There the similarity ended. They would travel fundamentally different paths through life, and their contrasting experiences serve to illustrate the conflicting expectations that Americans of this period had of their government and the new political order. Both Shays and Hamilton fought for national independence and individual liberty during the Revolution, but they held widely differing notions as to what these concepts meant. Hamilton may have liked to think that he rose by virtue of talent and merit alone, but he derived great advantage along the way from the favors bestowed and the assistance rendered by men of wealth, power, and distinction. As an influential member of the postrevolutionary elite, he was both defender and beneficiary of the newly established social and political order. Hamilton had little respect or regard for the ordinary citizen. In a speech be made to the Constitutional Convention in 1787 he observed that, "the voice of the people has been said to be the voice of God, but it is not true in fact. The people are turbulent and ever changing; they seldom judge or determine right."

Daniel Shays was an outsider. Like other members of his class he was a debtor rather than a creditor, a common man rather than an educated gentleman, a laborer rather than a wealthy merchant or speculator or landowner. These different classes of Americans, represented in one instance by Daniel Shays and in the other by Alexander Hamilton, had different needs and interests. It was these different interests—and the differing expectations with respect to what government should do about them—that gave rise to the conflicts and frustrations of the decade of the 1780s. Out of these conditions would come the impetus and energy to lay a new political foundation to support the fledgling American Republic. Before we focus on the writing and ratification of the constitution, however, we need to return our attention to the frustrations and bitterness that produced Shays' Rebellion.

## STATE LEGISLATURES

It was not only the rebellion that had dismayed the revolutionary leaders and caused then to despair over the apparent corruption of republican values.[11] Ordinary citizens were also asserting their newly discovered power and authority in other ways. The most significant development in this regard was the democratization of state legislatures. In 1765, for example, the colonial legislature in New Hampshire was dominated by members of the landed gentry. By 1786, most of its members were small farmers and men of only moderate wealth. Before the Revolutionary War, wealthy men comprised 83 percent of the membership in the New York and New Jersey legislatures. After the War, they accounted for only 38 percent of the membership.[12] In Maryland, South Carolina, and Virginia, the upper class held more than half the legislative seats before the war. Afterwards, they accounted for only one in every four. In Massachusetts, candidates sympathetic to the grievances that had produced Shays' Rebellion won control of the state legislature in Boston. In Rhode Island, during 1783–1785, the legislature was dominated by a coalition of artisans, craftsmen, and small farmers. In Pennsylvania, the new constitution established a unicameral legislature that dominated the state government. The courts had limited power and the executive could not veto laws passed by the legislature. Legislators had to run for election every year and members could not serve for more than four years out of every seven. They also had to take an oath to protect the interests of the "people." All legislative proceedings were open to the

---

[11] John D. Riggins, *The Lost Soul of American Politics* (New York: Basic Books, 1984).
[12] Wood, *The Radicalism of the American Revolution*.

public and proposed bills had to be printed "for the consideration of the people" before they could become law.

## Radical Democracy

In general, state legislatures became more democratic as a result of the Revolution. They were highly representative of ordinary citizens, were periodically reapportioned, and in some states constituents were even permitted to issue voting instructions to their representatives. Not only were elections held annually, but the turnover of incumbents each year frequently exceeded half of the total membership. In short, these elected representatives were highly responsive to their constituents. But how, asked the revolutionary leaders, could elected officials act in the public interest if they were beholden to narrow, private interests? According to Ezra Stiles, president of Yale College, such a representative looks at each new piece of legislation and "instantly thinks how it will affect his constituents. Instead of electing men to office for their abilities, integrity and patriotism, the people vote from some mean, interested, or capricious motive. They choose a man because he will vote for a new town, or a new county, or in favor of a memorial; because he is noisy in blaming those who are in office, . . . or because he possesses in a superiment degree, the all-prevailing popular talent of coaxing and flattering." According to this perspective, ordinary men elected by and beholden to other ordinary men could never possess the republican virtue essential to governing in the public rather than the private interest. Only the select few could "look down with contempt upon every mean or interested pursuit; only a few were liberally educated and cosmopolitan enough to have the breadth of perspective to comprehend all the different interests of the society; and only a few were independent and unbiased enough to adjudicate among these different interests and advance the public rather than a private good."[13]

## Radical Laws

But what really alarmed the elite were the types of laws these popular legislatures were enacting. They passed legislation that authorized the issuing of paper currency, that provided for debtor relief, and that routinely violated legal contracts. They enacted, amended, and abolished laws on a continuous basis and with what appeared to be little logic or reason. The legislatures dominated government in their respective states. They exercised judicial and executive as well as legislative authority. Governors were essentially powerless. As the supreme center of power, the legislatures involved themselves in even the mundane and bureaucratic aspects of government. They heard and resolved complaints and problems brought by individual citizens, they passed judgment on

[13] *Ibid.*

the legality of land titles, they granted divorces, and even suspended fines and sentences. According to the elite, they had essentially gotten out of hand. The legislatures had become too powerful. Responsiveness to the people was one thing. But when the legislature violated contracts and issued an endless supply of paper currency it was mounting an attack upon private property. When it usurped executive and judicial power and passed laws that infringed upon the basic rights of individual citizens, it was engaged in an assault on liberty itself. James Madison observed these legislatures at work and wrote that "the people were as capable of despotism as any prince; public liberty was no guarantee after all of private liberty." According to Madison it was now apparent that the many had little to fear from the powerful few. Instead, "It is much more to be dreaded that the few will be unnecessarily sacrificed to the many."

## DIRECT DEMOCRACY

This elite fear of the "tyranny of the majority" was not a false concern. In fact, developments were under way which indicate that even more frightening tendencies were at work in the political system. Why, some of the radical political leaders asked, should the power of the people end with an elected legislature? James Burgh wrote that "In planning a government by representation, the people ought to provide against their own annihilation. They ought to establish a regular and constitutional method of action by and from themselves, without, or even in opposition to their representatives, if necessary." Samuel Adams argued that the people had the right "to assemble upon all occasions to consult measures for promoting liberty and happiness." In fact, these were arguments for a pure and unadulterated democracy. The people were "the sole lawful legislature," and every man was a "co-legislator with all the other members of the community." According to this interpretation of political power and authority, only the people were the final arbiters of the laws under which they would live. Laws enacted by the legislature had validity only to the extent that the people approved of them. It was not up to the judiciary to determine the legitimacy of a particular law. It was not even necessary for the voters to elect a new set of representatives to revoke a previously enacted and distasteful piece of legislation. Instead, "a majority of the people at large have a right to reverse and annul every act and contract of all the legislatures on the continent." An act of the legislature would stand as a valid law to be obeyed only if the people did not object to it. Ultimate political power rested with the people, and it was a power they could exercise directly and frequently.

## ELITE FEARS

Not surprisingly, the elite were alarmed by these arguments. Where was there a decisive role for the virtuous, educated, and enlightened gentleman in such a political arrangement? Gentlemen of merit, distinction, and talent would be overwhelmed by the self-interested masses under such conditions. Assaults on the individual liberties and private property of the minority by a tyrannical majority were inevitable. Government would serve the private self-interest of the many rather than the public interest of the whole. According to one critic, "so long as the people shall be impressed with the idea that they can, at any time constitutionally control and direct the legislature, they will be appealed to for that reason."

It was not just the political rhetoric of a few radical politicians that frightened those revolutionary leaders who had envisioned a republic based on virtue and the rejection of narrow self-interest. Remember that state legislatures throughout the nation had already passed laws that violated contracts, provided for the printing of paper currency, and suspended the implementation of a variety of legal measures designed to ensure the collection of debts by creditors. Beyond that, citizens' conventions and committees were meeting regularly throughout the New England states during the 1780s. Riots broke out in a number of cities. The new constitution in Pennsylvania even provided for a "Council of Censors," an elected body which had the authority to examine the performance of the government and call a new constitutional convention if it so desired.

It is in this light that the elite reaction to Shays' Rebellion—as well as the reaction to the farmer rebellions that occurred in other states—should be evaluated. The very future of the American Republic was thought to be at stake. The people increasingly—rather than a despot—seemed to be the most likely

The Battle of Lexington during the Revolutionary War. (Credit: The Granger Collection, New York)

source of tyranny. In today's America, where government seems distant and even alien, where elected representative are much better educated and considerably more wealthy than their constituents, where congress is dominated by committees composed of long-time incumbents who are returned to office with monotonous regularity in elections where many of the citizens don't even bother to vote, and where laws are made in an environment far removed from the scrutiny and participation of the ordinary citizen, it is hard to imagine that the generation of the American Revolution did, in fact, directly and energetically participate in political affairs. That is why the decades of the 1770s and 1780s are so crucial to an understanding of why the Constitution was written, and why it provided for one particular form of government rather than another. The document that emerged from the convention in Philadelphia was powerfully shaped and fashioned by the political events and developments that followed the Revolution. The Constitution that we live under today did not emerge full-blown from the unbiased political imaginations and genius of the founding fathers. Instead, it reflects an imperfect understanding of the conflicts, fears and aspirations of the post-war years. The revolutionary leaders had envisioned a republic that rested on a solid foundation of virtue, governed by leaders recruited from an "aristocracy of talent," and dedicated to the pursuit of the public interest. But the optimism of the revolutionary years quickly gave way to a deepseated pessimism. The radicalism of the state legislatures, the legislative assaults on private property and individual liberty, and the rejection of republican virtue in favor of the pursuit of narrow self-interest, convinced the elite that the passions of the people recognized few restraints. If disgruntled common citizens could take up arms against duly constituted public authority—as in the case of Shays' Rebellion—if the national government under the Articles of Confederation was too enfeebled to take action against them, and if these defeated rebels could then rally their followers and gain control of the state legislature through the sheer weight of numbers, then the hope that a republic based on virtue and public interest could survive was nonsense. The people themselves were now seen as the gravest threat to liberty. James Madison thought that the greatest danger lay not in what the few would do to the many, but in what the many would do to the few. Governor Morris put it more bluntly when he observed of the people, "Poor reptiles! They bask in the sun, and ere noon they will bite, depend upon it." What kind of government would be created by men who had so low a regard for the common man? In Chapter 3 we shall see, for the Constitution would be written by men like Madison and Hamilton and Adams, the latter of whom had observed that the people "can neither act, judge, think or will." It would not be framed by Daniel Shays or Samuel Adams. Not a single ordinary citizen would attend the Convention as a delegate. The new government would be designed by men who came equipped with a powerful and clearly defined set of perspectives and biases. But even some members of the elite would grow uncomfortable with what they had done. In 1788, Richard Henry Lee of Virginia wrote,

> It will be considered, I believe, as a most extraordinary epoch in the history of mankind, that in a few years there should be so essential a change in the minds of men. Tis really astonishing that the same people, who have just emerged from a long and cruel war in defense of liberty, should now agree to fix an elective despotism upon themselves and their posterity.[14] (p. 297)

## RECOMMENDED READINGS

Cooke, Jacob E. 1982. *Alexander Hamilton.* New York: Charles Scribners.
Diggins, John D. 1984. *The Lost Soul of American Politics.* New York: Basic Books.
Middlekauff, Robert. 1982. *The Glorious Cause.* New York: Oxford University Press.
Morone, James A. 1990. *The Democratic Wish.* New York: Basic Books.
Severo, Richard and Lewis Milford. 1989. *The Wages of War.* New York: Simon & Schuster.
Wood, Gordon S. 1969. *The Creation of the American Republic.* Chapel Hill: University of North Carolina Press.
Wood, Gordon S. 1992. *The Radicalism of the American Revolution.* New York: Knopf.

---

[14] *Ibid.*

# 3

# *The Constitution*

| | |
|---|---|
| The Opening Shot | The Importance of Property |
| Madison Takes the Offensive | The Federalist, No. 10 |
| The Reaction | Maintaining the Spirit and Form |
| The Constitution Takes Shape | Ratification |
| Idealism or Economics | Antifederalists |
| Economic Powers |     *Antifederalist Criticisms* |
| Something for Everyone | The State Conventions |
| Military Powers | New York |
| National Supremacy | The Legacy of Ratification |
| In Defense of the Framers | Conclusion |

> The vile State governments are the sources of pollution, which will contaminate the American name for ages, Smite them, smite them, in the name of God and the people.
>
> —Henry Knox

> I smelt a Rat.
>
> —Richard Henry Lee

Richard Henry Lee had been selected as a delegate to the Constitutional Convention by the Virginia legislature, but he refused to attend. He smelled something he did not like. Several other notables were also conspicuous by their absence. Samuel Adams was sick, Patrick Henry wanted no part of the proceedings, and Thomas Jefferson and John Adams were serving the government as ministers in Europe. But most of the stars of the revolutionary generation were there, meeting in May 1787 in Philadelphia, a city whose population of 30,000 made it the largest city in America. What would come out of the Constitutional Convention would shock many citizens. The *Federal Farmer* editorialized that if the people had anticipated what was about to happen, "Probably no state would have appointed members to the convention. Probably not one man in ten thousand in the United States had an idea that the old ship was to be destroyed."

The "old ship" had charted a course set by the Articles of Confederation, and although she had run hard aground on the shoals of political and economic turmoil, most expected the convention in Philadelphia to simply undertake repairs. Instead, the Articles were scuttled; they had provided only for a loose confederation among the states:

- Changes in the Articles required the consent of all 13 states.
- Major decisions required the approval of nine states.
- Each state had equal representation in Congress.
- Congress lacked the power to pass laws. Essentially, it was limited to enacting recommendations. It was up to the states to implement and enforce them.
- The Articles provided little in the way of executive, judicial, and administrative powers.

The power to make and enforce laws remained with the individual states. State governments were criticized for violating treaties, refusing to pay debts, interfering with the commerce and trade of other states, issuing paper currency, and refusing to pay their share of national expenses. The Confederation provided only for "a firm league of friendship," an alliance among individual states that essentially retained their independence and authority. The political system established by the Articles reflected the widespread fear of executive authority and a strong central government. In addition, Americans had been heavily influenced by Montesquieu who maintained that republican government required both a small territory and a small, homogeneous population. Since a republic depended upon the consent and support of the governed, it could not effectively function in societies that included a large number of conflicting interests.

However, powerful pressures were building to strengthen the Articles. Even its supporters recognized that the defects of the Confederation required attention. One criticism was directed against the Confederation's inability to legislate in the areas of public credit, finance, and taxation. At one point, the Confederation had even stopped paying interest on the national debt. By 1781, the Congress could no longer afford to pay expenses associated with printing its own proceedings. If the government could not even pay interest on the public debt, there was little likelihood that it would be able to borrow additional money. Robert Morris, the Superintendent of Finance, attempted to make the central government's bonds more attractive to investors by recommending that the Articles be amended to provide for a 5-percent duty on imported goods. However, Rhode Island and New York vetoed the proposal.

Another criticism focused on the Confederation's inability to regulate commerce. Merchants engaged in interstate trade, planters interested in the opening of foreign markets, and artisans and craftsmen who wanted tariffs levied on goods imported from abroad strongly supported giving Congress the power to regulate navigation, impose tariffs, protect domestic manufacturers, and retaliate against the unfair trade practices of other nations. An important initial step toward constitutional reform was taken in 1785 when representatives from Virginia and Maryland met at Mount Vernon to resolve their differences with respect to navigation on the Potomac River and Chesapeake Bay. This cooperative experience resulted in Virginia's invitation to the states to convene in Annapolis, Maryland, in 1786 to "recommend a federal plan for regulating commerce."

Still another area of criticism emphasized the Confederation's weakness in foreign affairs. Many Americans were outraged by the way the new Republic was being treated abroad. Unable to defend herself on the open seas, American ships were routinely seized by pirates from the North African states. The nation was further humiliated when the crews were sold into slavery. When the individual states under the Confederation failed to abide by their treaty obligations (which required them to return the property seized from Loyalist citizens during the Revolutionary War), the British retaliated by refusing to withdraw its military forces from the Northwest Territory. In addition, Spain closed the Mississippi River in 1784 to American navigation. This dispute with Spain—which also included the issue of opening Spanish territory to American trade—divided the northern and western states. Attempts to resolve the dispute through treaty negotiations failed when the southern states refused to provide the nine-state majority required under the Articles of Confederation. Increasingly, it appeared to many that the nation was on the verge of fragmenting into separate confederations over these differences.[1]

Pressure was growing, therefore, for a central government strong enough to regulate commerce; establish a stable currency and credit system; levy and collect taxes; defend American shipping on the high seas; enforce treaty obligations; provide for internal improvements such as harbors, roads, and canals; negotiate with foreign powers from a position of strength; control the disposal of western lands; and establish a national military force capable of protecting its citizens from the Indians as well as domestic insurrections.

As we have seen in Chapter 2, however, other powerful motivations existed as well. The decade was characterized by a struggle among various groups over the nature and control of public power. Many of the revolutionary leaders were growing increasingly apprehensive over the likely outcome of this

---

[1] Lance Benning, "From Confederation to Convention," *This Constitution* 6 (Spring: 1985), pp. 12–18.

struggle. The democratization of state legislatures, Shays' Rebellion, the enactment of radical state legislation that was perceived as an assault on liberty and property, direct citizen participation in political affairs through the mechanisms of conventions, committees, and associations, and the growing claim that ultimate sovereignty rested with the people, had deeply disturbed the members of the revolutionary elite. How could republican government endure among a people who lacked virtue, were prone to appeals to their basest passions, and who, in the mad scramble after individual self-interest, left political turmoil in their wake? According to this perspective, the deliberations of the Constitutional Convention were about more than just strengthening the powers of the central government in areas ranging from commerce and currency to taxation and foreign affairs. The fundamental issue grappled with by the delegates revolved around the following questions: Can republican government endure in this nation? Can public institutions be created that will ensure the survival of republican principles in spite of the base tendencies of the people? The Constitutional Convention was as much concerned with human nature and human emotion as it was with trade and taxes.

## THE OPENING SHOT

The growing momentum to strengthen the national government led to a call of the states to meet in Annapolis, Maryland, in 1786 to address tax and tariff issues. Although only 12 delegates from five states attended, the meeting did accomplish one very important piece of business. Under the leadership of James Madison, the delegates urged Congress to issue a call for a convention of the states to review and revise the Articles of Confederation. Congress responded by passing a resolution in February 1787, calling for such a convention, with the express purpose of revising the Articles and making them "adequate to the exigencies of government and the preservation of the Union."

When the 55 delegates from 12 states finally got down to business on May 25, 1787, they elected George Washington as their presiding officer, decided that each state would have one vote, and further agreed that decisions would be made by majority vote. They were an elite group, well-educated for the most part, and young (forty-two was the average age). They also represented a huge reservoir of political experience. Several had participated in state constitutional conventions, no less than seven had served as governors of their states, and 39 had been elected to Congress. A third of them were veterans of the Revolutionary Army. Thirty-four of them were lawyers.

## MADISON TAKES THE OFFENSIVE

James Madison and the Virginia delegation shocked the delegates with the introduction of the Virginia Plan. Madison proposed nothing less than throwing out the Articles of Confederation, and replacing them with a powerful central government. The new government would consist of a single executive, a bicameral legislature, and a judicial branch. The executive would be selected by the national legislature for a single term, with the judiciary chosen by the legislature as well. While the lower House of the legislature would be elected directly by the people, members of the upper House would be chosen by the lower House from persons nominated by the states. A veto power over the acts of both the national legislature and state legislatures would be vested in a "Council of Revision," which would consist of the executive and members of the national judiciary.

James Madison. (Source: White House Historical Association)

The most startling part of the Virginia Plan dealt with state power. The Virginia Plan called for "a strong consolidated union, in which the idea of states should be nearly annihilated." The national legislature would not only have the power to legislate "in all cases to which the states are incompetent," it would also have the power to veto or "to negate all laws passed by the several states." Madison's deep distrust of—and contempt for—state power is never more obvious than in this proposal. If Madison had his way, the national government would exercise double veto power over the states. The first would be lodged in the "Council of Revision," while the second would be held by the national legislature. The Virginia Plan called for a fundamental reordering of political power and authority in the nation. Essentially, Madison's scheme would have the national government bypass the states, and exercise political authority directly over individual citizens.

## THE REACTION

Substantial opposition to the Virginia Plan was quick in coming. William Patterson of New Jersey argued that the provision requiring that both Houses of the national legislature be selected according to proportional representation was unacceptable. Proportional representation would benefit the larger states and penalize the smaller ones. Patterson maintained that New Jersey would never accept such an arrangement. The Pennsylvania delegation responded by claiming that they would never accept a government in which each state had equal representation. The stage was now set for a major vote on the issue. On June 11, the delegates decided to accept Madison's proposal calling for proportional representation in both Houses. However, the opponents of proportional representation took heart from the fact that they lost the vote on the upper House by the slimmest of margins (six states to five).

Encouraged by the narrow defeat on proportional representation, Patterson now introduced a series of proposals that became known as the New Jersey Plan. Patterson's resolutions consisted of a series of amendments to the Articles of Confederation. Under this arrangement, each state would retain equal representation. However, the national legislature (Congress) would be given very considerable powers to tax and regulate commerce. The Convention was now at an impasse. In addition to New Jersey, Connecticut, New York, and Delaware supported Patterson's compromise proposal. Opposition to the Virginia Plan had solidified. It was now apparent that some of the state delegations would never agree to Madison's proposal to grossly reduce the role of the states.

The debate now shifted to the role of the states in the new government. A successful resolution of the issues that divided the delegates was far from assured. In fact, one delegate observed that the convention was "scarce held together by the strength of a hair." The controversy over the representation of the states extended beyond the issue of large states versus small ones. Madison's opposition to equal representation of the states in the Congress was based on more than the fact that he was a delegate from a large state. It also stemmed from the belief that the states had been the primary cause of the troubles experienced under the Articles of Confederation. If the states were given equal representation in the new government, similar difficulties could be anticipated.

Many of the delegates agreed with this strong nationalist perspective. But not enough. On July 16, the Connecticut Compromise was approved by a vote of six states to four with one divided. Each state would be represented by two senators in the upper House.

## THE CONSTITUTION TAKES SHAPE

The decision to provide the states with equal representation in the Senate fundamentally altered the thrust of the Virginia Plan. In place of an essentially omnipotent national legislature, the Convention now moved to assign the Congress a specific set of powers. Instead of a national veto over state laws, the delegates decided to specify a series of prohibitions upon state behavior. The states were prohibited from levying duties on imports and exports, from coining money and issuing paper currency, from entering into treaties, from enacting bills of attainder and ex post facto laws, and from impairing the obligations of contracts. These restrictions upon state power were highly significant. In large measure, the prohibitions specified in what would eventually become Article I, Section 10 of the Constitution prevented the states from engaging in the types of activities and behavior that had so troubled and unsettled the revolutionary leaders. States could no longer pass laws that voided contractual obligations between debtors and creditors. They were specifically prevented from issuing paper currency by the stipulation that they could not "make anything but gold and silver coin a tender in payment of debts." They were forbidden from entering into any alliance with another state. They were also denied a primary revenue source by the prohibition against the levying of taxes on imports and exports.

Another consequence of the defeat suffered by the nationalists as a result of the vote on the Connecticut Compromise was reflected in the deliberations regarding the executive. Originally, the Senate had been given exclusive power to make treaties and appoint ambassadors and justices of the Supreme Court. However, the decision to give each state equal representation in the Senate caused Madison and the nationalists to rethink their position on the issue. As a result, these powers were transferred to the executive. The Senate was relegated to the role of advising and consenting. Similarly, the Connecticut Compromise also influenced the method devised to select the president. The nationalists were apprehensive about having the president selected by a congress in which Senate membership would be apportioned equally among the states. Opposition also arose to a proposal that the president be limited to a single seven-year term, as well as to a plan whereby the executive would be elected directly by the people. Eventually, the delegates settled upon the electoral college. It was a compromise that effectively addressed a number of concerns raised by the delegates. First, by removing the selection of the president from the control of the Congress, it maintained the independence of the chief executive without limiting the number of terms he could serve. Second, the electoral college was essentially a carbon copy of the Congress. Therefore, its composition satisfied the nationalists as well as the delegates representing the small states.[2]

## IDEALISM OR ECONOMICS

Were the framers of the Constitution motivated by a desire to protect and preserve republican government? Did they labor in Philadelphia to ensure that the American Republic would endure as "a new order of the ages"? Or were they a powerful, propertied elite primarily motivated by an intent to protect and advance their own economic interests?

---

[2] Calvin Jillson and Cecil L. Eubanks, "The Political Structure of Constitution Making: The Federal Convention of 1787," *American Political Science Review 28* (August: 1984).

According to one perspective, the framers sought to establish a new political order that would nurture public virtue and protect republican government. The rampant self-interest of the masses, the radicalism of the state legislatures, the tyranny of the majority, and the spectre of Shays' Rebellion served as powerful reminders of the fate that had historically befallen experiments in republican government. The founding fathers were high-minded men who were little interested in realizing personal gain from the new constitutional order. Instead, they were motivated primarily by the desire to perpetuate republican principles and institutions. The other interpretation of the framers' intentions is less laudatory. According to Charles A. Beard, "the members of the Philadelphia Convention which drafted the Constitution were, with few exceptions, immediately, directly, and personally interested in, and derived economic advantage from, the establishment of the new system."[3]

Those who believe that the founding fathers were primarily motivated by economic interest point to a variety of evidence in support of their argument. They note that James Madison was quite explicit in *Federalist—Number 10* regarding the dominance of class and economic interests. According to Madison, those without property constituted "the majority faction." He went on to write that,

> ... the most common and durable source of factions has been the various and unequal distribution of property. Those who hold and those who are without property have ever formed distinct interests in society. Those who are creditors and those who are debtors fall under like discrimination. A landed interest, a manufacturing interest, a mercantile interest, a monied interest, with many lesser interests, grow up of necessity in civilized nations, and divide them into different classes, actuated by different sentiments and views.[4]

But Madison went further than that. He warned against the "leveling impulses" of this property-less faction, and argued that, "To secure the public good and private rights against the danger of such a faction and at the same time preserve the spirit and form of popular government is then the great object to which our inquiries are directed." To critics, this passage represents the proverbial smoking gun. For them, the evidence is compelling. The premeditated intent of the framers was to create a political system that would weaken the influence of the masses and protect and enhance the political power and economic interests of the elite. Only the "spirit and form of

---

[3] Charles A. Beard, *An Economic Interpretation of the Constitution of the United States* (New York: Macmillan, 1913).
[4] Alexander Hamilton, James Madison, and John Jay, *The Federalist Papers* (Baltimore: Johns Hopkins University Press, 1981).

popular government" would be honored. The substance and content would be rendered hollow.[5]

## ECONOMIC POWERS

Critics argue that a number of sections in the Constitution clearly illustrate how the framers designed a document explicitly intended to benefit the class and economic interests of the elite. In Article I, Section 8, for example, the new Congress is given the power to levy taxes, borrow money, regulate commerce, coin money, regulate its value, and establish laws regarding bankruptcies throughout the nation. Critics maintain that by removing these powers from the states and giving them to the national government, the framers enhanced the control of the merchant, banking, and investor class over commerce, currency, and credit. No longer would these vital economic issues be subjected to the whim and radicalism of the thirteen individual state legislatures. By assigning these powers to the new national government and removing them from the control of popularly elected state legislatures, the elite sought to minimize the assaults on property that had characterized the decade of the 1780s.

## SOMETHING FOR EVERYONE

Critics charge that practically every group of elites was granted special benefits, favors, and protection under the new Constitution. Land speculators were taken care of by a provision that gave Congress the "Power to dispose of and make all needful Rules and Regulations respecting the Territory or other property belonging to the United States." In turn, speculators in securities issued by the government under the Articles of Confederation were protected by Article VI which provided that "All debts contracted and Engagements entered into, before the Adoption of this Constitution, shall be as valid against the United States under this Constitution, as under the Confederation." Creditors were also singled out as deserving of special attention. The states were specifically prohibited from issuing paper money. In addition, they were now prevented from accepting "anything but gold and silver coin as Tender in Payment of Debts." Finally, the states were prohibited from passing any law "impairing the obligation of contracts." The constitutional provisions that prohibited the states from issuing paper currency, that limited the payment of debts to gold and silver, and that prevented the impairing of contracts, bestowed distinct benefits on creditors at the expense of debtors.

---

[5] Michael Parneti, "The Constitution as an Elitist Document," in Robert A. Goldwin and William A. Schambra, (Eds.), *How Democratic Is the Constitution?* (Washington, DC: American Enterprise Institute, 1980).

Slaveholders were also successful in arranging constitutional protection for their property. In fact, a compromise was reached whereby three-fifths of the slaves in each state would be counted in the determination of both representation and the apportionment of direct taxes. Further, the Constitution provided that "No Person held to Service or Labor in one State under the laws thereof, escaping into another shall . . . be discharged from such Service or Labor, but shall be delivered up on claim of the Party to whom such Service or Labor be due." Although Congress was authorized to abolish the slave trade after 1808, slaveholders were given ample opportunity to obtain a plentiful supply of slaves before the ban was imposed.

## MILITARY POWERS

Those who believe that the Constitution was written to protect the economic and class interests of the elite from repeated assaults by popular majorities and radical state legislatures point to the military powers given to the new national government as further evidence in support of their argument. The framers were not only fearful of rebellious farmers, they were also frightened by the prospects of slave revolts. In *The Federalist,* James Madison observes that under normal circumstances slaves "were sunk below the level of men." However, he was apprehensive that under "the tempestuous seeds of civil violence [they] may emerge into human character and give a superiority of strength to any party with which they may associate themselves." The clear implication is that the framers were frightened by the prospect of an alliance among rebellious farmers, debtors, and slaves. The radical state legislatures—beset by passions, factions, and wild schemes, and under the control of popular majorities—could not be depended upon to maintain law and order and protect liberty and property from the tyranny of the many. The solution was to provide the national government with the means to preserve stability and "republican" government. Specifically, Congress is given the power in Article I, Section 8 to:

- Raise and support armies.
- Provide for calling forth the Militia to execute the Laws of the Union, suppress Insurrections and repel invasions.
- Provide for organizing, arming and disciplining the Militia, and for governing such part of them as may be employed in the Service of the United States.
- Erect forts, magazines, and arsenals.
- To make all laws which shall be necessary and proper for carrying into execution the foregoing powers.

Further, Article II, Section 2, provides that "The President shall be Commander-in-Chief of the Army and Navy of the United States, and of the Militia of the several states, when called into the actual service of the United States." Finally, Article IV, Section 4, stipulates that "The United States shall guarantee to every State in this Union a Republican Form of Government, and shall protect each of them against Invasion; and on application of the Legislature, or of the Executive (when the legislature cannot be convened) against domestic violence."

## NATIONAL SUPREMACY

The new national government no longer had to depend upon the states to reestablish order. Under the new constitution the national government had the power to call forth the militia to "suppress insurrections and repel invasions," "guarantee a republican form of government," protect each state against "domestic violence," and "execute the laws of the Union." When joined with the national supremacy clause, these constitutional provisions provided the new central government with potentially unlimited power and authority to intervene decisively in the states and suppress whatever activity might be deemed by national officials as constituting domestic violence, an invasion, or an insurrection. Article VII of the Constitution stipulates that,

> This constitution, and the laws of the United States which shall be made in pursuance therefore; all treaties made, or which shall be made under the authority of the United States, shall be the supreme law of the land, and the judges of every state shall be bound thereby, anything in the Constitution or laws of any state to the contrary notwithstanding.

## IN DEFENSE OF THE FRAMERS

To others, the criticism that the delegates were motivated primarily by a need to protect and nurture their economic interests underestimates the complexity of the task facing the convention. Further, it fails to appreciate the variety of different goals that motivated the framers. Certainly, the delegates had class and economic interests. Surely, these considerations were reflected to some extent in their deliberations and decisions. To maintain, however, that explicitly economic interests were foremost in the framers' minds is incorrect. Surely, economic issues played a major role in the constitutional debate. It is misleading, however, to conclude that the delegates primarily sought to realize personal economic gain from their choices.[6]

---

[6] David E. Smith, *The Convention and the Constitution: The Political Ideas of the Founding Fathers* (New York: St. Martin's Press, 1965).

It will be recalled that a number of problems and issues had led to the calling of the Convention. First, there was widespread agreement that the Articles of Confederation were insufficient to the task of governing the new nation. Enfeebled by its inability to pass legislation providing for the most basic functions of government, and largely at the mercy of the individual states, the central government under the Articles presided over little more than "a firm league of friendship." These weaknesses produced outcomes that had consequences for ordinary citizens as well as the elite. For example, both rich and poor citizens had been outraged by the piracy of American ships on the high seas. Insults to national pride and honor cut across class and economic lines. Sentiment had also grown among a variety of different groups and classes to equip the national government with powers adequate to the tasks of defense, regulation of commerce, taxation, and the establishment of a sound currency and credit system. Both the well-off and ordinary citizen stood to benefit from a strong central government that could defend them against the Indians, build roads and bridges, enforce treaties, and regulate the disposal of Western lands.

Another powerful impulse toward strengthening the central government was provided by the genuine and legitimate fear of the elite that the American experiment in republican government would be shortlived. Many had expressed deep concern over the "wild schemes" of the state legislatures. The passionate pursuit of narrow self-interest on the part of ordinary citizens had convinced many that tyranny by the majority was a distinct rather than remote possibility. According to this perspective, the framers acted to preserve republican government for a people who lacked sufficient "virtue" to ensure it on their own.

Other defenders of the framers' intentions have noted that the Constitution left many state powers essentially intact. Although they lost the power to tax imports and exports, to coin money, to impair contracts, and to accept paper currency in payment of debts, they retained a wide and formidable array of functions and powers. These included the regulation of property, control over police powers, regulation of banking, insurance, and local government, responsibility for voting, elections, and political parties, administration of criminal, family, business, and consumer law, regulation of professions and occupations, adjudication of civil disputes, and responsibility for the provision of a variety of essential services ranging from education, health, and welfare to police protection, prisons, and sanitation.

The delegates seemed intent on removing the most contentious, divisive, and acrimonious issues from the realm and arena of localistic politics—contracts between creditors and debtors, taxing imports and exports, paper currency. Issues and areas thought less likely to inflame passions and threaten the foundations of republican government were left to the control of the states. Certainly, these constitutional prohibitions on state behavior conferred substantial advantage on the economic elite. Two points are relevant, however.

First, it can be argued that the *intent* on the part of the framers was political rather than economic. They were primarily concerned with curbing those tendencies toward radicalism that might corrupt republican principles. One way to achieve this goal was to remove from state control the power to resolve the most divisive issues—debtor relief, taxation, paper currency, the regulation of commerce.

Second, it could be argued that if the framers were primarily motivated by a need to protect and advance the economic interests of the elite, why did they leave so much power in the hands of the states? Indeed, the delegates seemed to be remarkably unconcerned, for the most part, with the internal affairs of the states. The states retained their police powers as well as their authority to regulate everything from property and business to voting, elections, and legal procedures. Certainly, most of the powers retained by the states were directly relevant to both conferring benefits and imposing burdens on the business and propertied classes. That the framers left these powers essentially intact and under the jurisdiction of the states implies that political rather than economic motives may well have guided their choices.

## THE IMPORTANCE OF PROPERTY

The protection of property was, however, of enormous importance to the framers. Few would have argued with Governor Morris' contention that the protection of property was the "principal object of government." Proponents of an economic interpretation of the Constitution have pointed to this assumption regarding the appropriate ends of public power as further evidence in support of their argument. It will be recalled from Chapter 2, however, that the concept of property occupied a special place in the mindset of these "first generation gentlemen." One of their primary objections to the control exerted over state legislatures by groups of ordinary citizens was that men who had to constantly scramble to make a living were poorly equipped to govern in the public interest. The unending pursuit of self-interest, and the frantic competition to eke out a living and best one's neighbor, inevitably corrupted the ordinary man and rendered him unfit to perform the civic duties of a virtuous citizen.

The mass of men were ill-equipped to provide leadership in a republic, not because they suffered from a basic defect of character or personality, but because the precarious nature of their economic circumstances reduced them to engaging in a continuous struggle. This perspective on human behavior held by the framers should help us understand why the protection of property assumed such vital significance for them. They sought to establish constitutional safeguards not simply to enrich themselves, but to guarantee protection for that property upon which both virtue and liberty depended. If ordinary men were incapable of setting aside their self-interest, then the duties and obligations of republican government would descend upon "enlightened gentlemen" of property. The problem for the framers was that the experience of the decade preceding the Constitutional Convention revealed that the masses of ordinary men were unwilling to defer to the enlightened political judgment of those gentlemen who composed this "aristocracy of talent." Instead, they rapidly became accustomed to the notion that they were quite capable of governing themselves. Ordinary citizens seized upon the radical idea that the leadership of a virtuous elite governing in the public interest was unnecessary. In fact, the appropriate end of government was to help ordinary men achieve their private purposes. Elite reaction to this perspective was reflected in the framers deepening fear of the "tyranny of the majority."

## THE FEDERALIST, NO. 10

Nowhere is this perceived threat to republican principles at the hands of popular majorities more effectively expressed and analyzed than in Madison's *Federalist No. 10*. This writing represents one of the most important documents in American political history. It also provides enormous insight with respect to the motivations and intentions of the framers. Therefore, it deserves careful scrutiny. In *The Federalist,* Madison offers his now famous definition of "faction," as a number of citizens "who are united and actuated by some common impulse of passion, or of interest, adverse to the rights of other citizens, or to the permanent and aggregate interests of the community":

> A zeal for different opinions concerning religion, concerning government, . . . an attachment to different leaders ambitiously contending for preeminence and power . . . have, in turn, divided mankind into parties, inflamed them with mutual animosity, and rendered them much more disposed to vex and oppress each other, than to cooperate for their common good. So strong is this propensity of mankind, to fall into mutual animosities, that where no substantial occasion presents itself, the most frivolous and fanciful distinctions have been sufficient to kindle their unfriendly passions and excite their most violent conflicts. But the most common and durable source of factions, has been the various and unequal distribution of property. Those who hold, and those who are without property, have ever formed distinct interests in society . . . The regulation of these various and interfering interests forms the principal task of modern legislation . . .

In this passage, Madison suggests that it was not the protection of property per se that guided the structuring of constitutional power, but the regulation of those conflicting interests generated by the unequal division and control of that property. He further observes that a republican government can deal with a faction as long as it consists of less than a majority. The threat arises when a faction includes the majority. Then, the majority faction has the power to damage "both the public good and the rights of other citizens." For Madison, the principal objective of government becomes not the protection of property, but, "To secure the public good, and private rights, against the danger of a [majority] faction, and at the same time to preserve the spirit and form of popular government." Madison then argues that large republics are better able to control majority factions than small republics. This section is significant in that it reveals the basis of his strong attachment to a powerful national union and his unyielding opposition to the states:

> The smaller the society, the fewer probably will be the distinct parties and interests composing it, the fewer the parties and interests, the more frequently will a majority be found of the same party; and the smaller the number of individuals composing a majority, and the smaller the compass within which they are placed the more easily will they concert and execute their plans of oppression. Extend the sphere, and you take in a greater variety of parties and interests, you make it less probable that a majority of the whole will have a common motive to invade the rights of other citizens, or if such a common motive exists, it will be more difficult for all who feel it to discover their own strength, and to act in unison with each other.

Shays' Rebellion and the radical state legislatures represented distinct guideposts for Madison during the writing of *Federalist No. 10*. His fear of insurrection, as well as his concern with the divisive effects of the debtor/paper currency issue, are strongly evident in the following passage:

> The influence of factious leaders may kindle a flame within their particular states, but will be unable to spread a general conflagration through the other states . . . A rage for paper money, for an abolition of debts, for an equal division of property, or for any other improper or wicked project, will be less apt to pervade the whole body of the union than a particular member of it . . .

## MAINTAINING THE SPIRIT AND FORM

Madison defined the task of government as securing "the public good and private rights" against a majority faction, while, at the same time, maintaining "the spirit and form of popular government." How was this to be accomplished? One way it would be achieved was by removing direct control of government from the reach of popular majorities. The president would be selected by the electoral college, senators would be elected by their respective state legislatures, and judges were to be nominated by the president and approved by the Senate. Further, senators would serve six-year terms and judges would enjoy tenure for life. Only members of the House of Representatives would be elected directly by the people and serve short terms (two years). Even here, however, insuring accountability to the voters would be difficult to realize. Because of the small number of representatives, a single member of the House would represent 30,000 constituents. In fact, the House would have fewer members than all but two of the state legislatures. Patrick Henry feared that as a result the new system would favor the election of men of "conspicuous military, popular, civil, or legal talents."

Another obstacle placed in the path of majority factions took the form of separating the legislature, executive, and judicial branches. Since each enjoys a considerable measure of independence from others, a majority faction would find it exceedingly difficult to attain control over the entire machinery of government. Further, checks and balances are also employed to curb and frustrate majority desires.

1. The House and Senate each have the power to veto legislation passed by the other.
2. The Congress exercises control over the budget prepared by the president, can enact legislation over the president's veto, and has the power to impeach and convict the president.
3. The Senate approves presidential nominations to the judiciary, and the Congress is given the power to impeach and remove judges.
4. The president can veto laws passed by Congress.
5. The president nominates judges.

According to Madison, "Ambition must be made to counteract ambition."

## RATIFICATION

In the end, the score would be 13 to 0 in favor of ratification. But as is the case in many contests, the final score was not an accurate reflection of how much in doubt the outcome was until the very end. Ratification would ultimately prove to be a function of a variety of factors. These included the superior organizational skills and resources of the Federalists (those who supported adoption), as well as their success in ensuring that popularly elected conventions in each state rather than individual state legislatures would undertake the ratification issue. The political stature and reputation of the Federalists also had an impact. In the key state of Virginia, for example, George Washington and James Madison likely saved the day for the new Constitution. The powerful intellects of key supporters also contributed to a favorable outcome. Hoping to do just that, James Madison, Alexander Hamilton, and John Jay wrote a series of articles in defense of the Constitution that came to be known as the *Federalist Papers*. Regarded today as among the most important documents in American

**TABLE 3.1** Powers of the Congress

"All legislative Powers herein granted shall be vested in a Congress of the United States, which shall consist of a Senate and House of Representatives. The House of Representatives shall be composed of members chosen every second year by the People of the several states . . . The Senate of the United States shall be composed of two Senators from each state, chosen by the Legislature thereof, for six years, and each Senator shall have one vote."

1. All Bills for raising Revenue shall originate in the House of Representatives.
2. Power to levy and collect taxes.
3. Pay debts.
4. Provide for the common defense.
5. Borrow money.
6. Regulate interstate commerce.
7. Pass laws to regulate bankruptcies.
8. Coin money and regulate its value.
9. Fix the standard of weights and measures.
10. Punish counterfeiting.
11. Establish post offices and roads.
12. Regulate patents and copyrights.
13. Establish tribunals inferior to the Supreme Court.
14. Punish piracy.
15. Declare war.
16. Raise and support armies and provide and maintain a navy.
17. Call forth the state militia to execute the laws, suppress insurrections and repel invasions.
18. To make all Laws which shall be necessary and proper for carrying into execution the foregoing powers.

political history, their cogent and even brilliant analysis of political relationships and human nature almost certainly convinced many to support the new government.

There were other factors at work as well. As we shall see, timing and even sheer chance played a role. However, there was another powerful motivation that forced even some of the Constitution's staunchest critics to eventually favor adoption. What was the alternative? Essentially everyone agreed that the Articles of Confederation were grossly inadequate to the task of governing. Securing the unanimous consent of all 13 states required for amendment was recognized as an impossibility. Many of those who opposed the new Constitution but supported union believed that to do nothing would lead to political turmoil. Eventually the union among the states would dissolve into a number of competing alliances and confederations. Once fragmented, it might be impossible to put back together again. Like Richard Henry Lee of Virginia, some opponents were forced to conclude, "this or nothing."

## ANTIFEDERALISTS

The Antifederalists were a mixed lot. There is evidence that their support was strongest among the small farming communities in the interior of the nation, while the Federalists enjoyed their greatest strength in the established towns and cities along the Atlantic seaboard. But the differences between the two factions were based on more than geographical location. Often, the Federalists and Antifederalists in a particular state (such as Virginia and New York) were similar in terms of wealth and class. Both were members of the elite. Gary Wills in his book *Inventing America* argues that it is wrong to claim that the Antifederalists were "the champions of democracy against privilege." Instead, "They were often men of established power within their states, who did not want to yield that power to a federal apparatus."

### Antifederalist Criticisms

There were, however, some significant areas of dispute between the two groups with respect to how political power should be structured and exercised in the new nation, including:[7]

1. The new government would be aristocratic and antirepublican.
2. The states would lose much of their power.
3. Political power would reside with a handful of national officials, many of whom would not be directly accountable to the people.
4. The president would be an "elected despot."
5. The delegates to the Constitutional Convention had violated their authority under the Articles of Confederation by proposing a completely new government.
6. The proceedings had been closed to the people.
7. Republican government could not survive in a vast nation.
8. The national government's control over the military was a threat to both the states and the individual.
9. The absence of a Bill of Rights was a powerful threat to liberty and freedom.
10. The number of representatives in the national legislature was far too small to provide adequate representation to the people.

[7] Gordon S. Wood, *The Creation of the American Republic: 1776–1787* (Chapel Hill: University of North Carolina Press, 1969).

## THE STATE CONVENTIONS

At first, it appeared as if the Constitution would be quickly and easily approved. Delaware took the lead and ratified the new government on December 7, 1787. Not a single dissenting vote was cast. The size of the state played a role in the speed with which it gave its stamp of approval. The tiny state felt vulnerable next to gigantic Pennsylvania.

The process of ratification took on a decidedly different cast in Pennsylvania. As soon as the Constitutional Convention adjourned in Philadelphia in September 1787, the Federalists took the Constitution to the state legislature (which was also about to adjourn). The Antifederalists moved to delay consideration until the next scheduled state elections. They hoped to win a majority in the new state legislature and thereby keep it from issuing a call for a state ratifying convention. When the Federalists moved ahead anyway, the Antifederalist representatives walked out. Now two members short of the quorum necessary to conduct business, the Constitution's supporters appeared to be stymied. Throwing gentlemanly behavior as well as caution to the wind, the Federalists rousted two Antifederalists from their beds the next morning, forcibly carried them into the legislative chamber, and kept them against their will until a call for a ratifying convention was proposed and passed. The Convention met in December and approved the Constitution.

New Jersey voted its unanimous approval a week later, and on the second day of the new year Georgia followed suit. The next week Connecticut also ratified. Georgia was strongly attracted by the promise of the new national government to provide protection against the Creek Indians, while Connecticut looked to the Constitution to provide protection from a different threat. Long dependent economically on New York, Connecticut sought relief under the constitutional provision assigning regulatory control over interstate and foreign commerce to the national Congress.

Massachusetts represented the first serious test of whether the new political order would be given a chance to work. The causes and consequences of Shays' abortive rebellion had deeply embittered delegates on both sides of the issue. Many of the powers assigned to the new national government and denied to the states by the proposed Constitution—paper currency, legal tender in payment of debts, the obligation of contracts, taxation, and the regulation of commerce—struck to the very core of the controversies that had generated such animosity and violence between debtors and creditors and small farmers and bankers. In retrospect, it is highly likely that there might well never have been a "United States of America" if a mere 10 votes out of the 355 that would be cast had gone one way rather than the other. The Federalists were well-aware that the outcome in Massachusetts was crucial to the success of their cause. As a result, they carefully picked their primary targets.

Their targets were two of the most famous and popular men of the era. Samuel Adams and John Hancock were enormously influential, and when they finally announced where they stood on ratification, they would undoubtedly carry many delegates with them. Samuel Adams, (who is today better known in some circles for the highly regarded beer that bears his name, the label of which declares him to be a "Brewer and Patriot"), was finally persuaded to support ratification with the promise that a Bill of Rights would be added to the Constitution. The route to Hancock's heart was paved with an apparent awareness of the man's ego and ambition. The Federalists whispered in his ear that since George Washington—a Virginian—would be the first president, a New Englander would be the logical choice to balance the new administration as vice president. Since he was the most prominent public figure in the region, it seemed assured that John Hancock would be that choice. Hancock declared for ratification, and Massachusetts approved the Constitution by the narrow margin of 187 to 168. History would record that Mr. Hancock did not get the job.

And then there were three. Maryland became the seventh state to ratify in April, 1787, and South Carolina became the eighth the next month. On the face of it, South Carolina appeared prime to reject the new government. Always a staunch supporter of states' rights, South Carolina seemed unlikely to willingly give up that state power and authority required as a condition of admittance to membership in the new union. However, she voted for ratification. Two factors account for this outcome. First, the state had suffered greatly during the Revolutionary War and had incurred a huge debt to boot. Since the Constitution provided that the new national government would assume responsibility for such debts, South Carolina had much to gain by voting for ratification. Second, whites in the state were beginning to grow uneasy over the huge slave population in their midst. The prospect of a slave revolt was a perpetual concern. Not only was the new national government admirably equipped with a formidable array of constitutional powers designed to suppress rebellions, insurrections, and domestic violence, it also had at its disposal the means (both a national military and control over state militias) to put those powers into effect. In addition, South Carolina had no reason to believe that a strong national government would represent a threat to slavery. In fact, the Constitution protected slavery. Further, the "Three-Fifths Compromise" guaranteed that slaves would be counted in those representation schemes based on population, while Article IV, Section 2, specifically guaranteed that "Persons held to Service or Labour" who escaped to another state "shall be delivered up on claim." In addition, slaveholders had a full two decades to import additional slaves before Congress would have the authority to abolish the slave trade. The state was also reassured by the Compromise which provided that each state would have two members in the Senate. Finally, the difficulty involved in amending the

Constitution provided additional reason for slaveholders to believe that their property was free from interference by the national government.

New Hampshire made it official. When she ratified in June 1787, the consent of the nine states necessary for approval had been obtained. In reality, however, New Hampshire made little difference. The "Big Two"—Virginia and New York—had not yet acted, and without them the new union had little likelihood of success. What happened next in their respective state ratifying conventions would determine America's political future.

The first showdown was in Virginia, the most populous state, and arguably the most important. Certainly, the stature of Virginia's statesmen was without parallel. The author of the Declaration of Independence—Thomas Jefferson—was a Virginian. The "architect" of the Constitution—James Madison—was a Virginian. The commander-in-chief of the Continental Army and the president of the Constitutional Convention—George Washington—was a Virginian. The quality of her civic life, as well as her contributions to the theory and practice of republican government, were unrivalled. Even her lesser lights were, or would be, among the most prominent and influential public men of their generation—Edmund Pendleton, Patrick Henry, George Mason, Edmund Randolph, John Marshall, Richard Henry Lee, James Monroe. If she rejected the new government, it was certain that North Carolina and Rhode Island, and likely New York as well, would refuse to join the proposed union. It is difficult to imagine how the fledgling political system ordained by the Constitution could long endure the inevitable trials and tribulations that lay ahead without the powerful moral and political authority conferred by the presence of this great state. Her course was crucial, just as it would be three-quarters of a century later when the issue at hand would be the dismemberment of the union, rather than the birth of it. In significant degree, the delegates to the Virginia ratifying convention held in their hands the power to bestow legitimacy upon—or withhold it from—the new American union.

The delegates to the Virginia ratifying convention came from as far away as the Ohio and Mississippi River Valleys, 86 of them Federalists, 80 of them Antifederalists. Patrick Henry, the leader of the Antifederalists, hammered away at several themes. First, he argued that a strong national government would assault individual liberty. Second, he sounded an alarm that would grow increasingly shrill during

Patrick Henry. (Credit: Archive Photos)

the next century. Join the union, cautioned Henry, and subject yourself to the dominance of the Northern states. He also repeatedly charged that the Constitutional Convention in Philadelphia had flagrantly violated its grant of authority which limited it to revising the Articles of Confederation. Again and again he attacked the Federalists. "Who authorized them to speak the language of *We, the People,* instead of *We, the States?* If the states be not the agents of this compact, it must be one great, consolidated, national government . . ." Repeatedly, Henry raised the spectre of an omnipotent central government dictating Virginia's affairs.

This was the patriot who had proclaimed during the Revolution, "Give me liberty or give me death," and there was precious little about this Constitution that he liked. Henry saw the president in the new government as a tyrant in the making. "If your American chief be a man of ambition and abilities," he observed, "how easy is it for him to render himself absolute! The Army is in his hands." He found the concept of a standing army controlled by the national government to be particularly repugnant, since it could execute the "commands of tyranny." Nor could he stomach the authority that the national government exerted over the state militia. "My great objection to this government," he declared, with all the eloquence and passion he could muster,

George Washington presides over the signing of the Constitution. (Source: National Archives)

"is that it does not leave us the means of defending our rights, or of waging war against tyrants. You will find all the strength of this country in the hands of your enemies."

His was more than a voice crying in the wilderness. In the end, 78 other voices joined with Henry in voting against this new political system that many saw as a repudiation of the very principles they had recently fought a long and bloody war for. But just as the physically unimposing James Madison had played a major intellectual and organizational role at the Philadelphia Convention, he performed a similar function at the Virginia Convention. To Henry's impassioned pleas and predictions of tyranny, Madison issued reassurances that the delegates had little to fear and much to gain through membership in the new union. Eighty-eight of them voted with Madison, not only because of the compelling logic of his cogent analyses, but in considerable degree because George Washington had sent a letter asking them to. Washington wrote the delegates that the only choice was, "The Constitution or disunion."

And so the Virginia Convention voted for union, but if a mere five votes had gone the other way there likely would not have been much of a union to join. Henry's words would prove to be prophetic. He had sounded the alarm regarding the dangers of merging Virginia's future with a powerful central government on the one hand, and with the Northern states on the other. For all of Madison's brilliance and keen insight into political relationships, it was Henry who would be favored with history's verdict. Less than 75 years later, his dire predictions would be repeated throughout the Southern states, at conventions called to destroy the union rather than create it. Then the halls of secession would ring with condemnations of the evils perpetuated by the national government and the Northern states. The litany of sins would include majoritarian tyranny, assaults on liberty and property, and attacks on states' rights. And this time, many more would heed the accusations.

## NEW YORK

Only New York now counted. If she stayed out, the union could probably avoid fatal damage. However, if she came in, many doubts as to its capacity to endure would be removed. New York represented very thick icing on the cake. The problem for the Federalists in the New York state ratifying convention was that they were outnumbered by the Antifederalists by a two to one margin. However, the timing was bad. New York had waited too long to act. By the time the state ratifying convention convened on June 26, 1788, it was too late. New Hampshire had ratified on June 21, and Virginia followed four days later. Suddenly, continued opposition to the Constitution on the part of many delegates seemed pointless. Nonetheless, the outcome was extremely close. The Constitution was approved by a vote of only 30 to 27.

## THE LEGACY OF RATIFICATION

In some states, the delegates to the ratifying conventions squarely confronted what the new political order would mean, and many did not like what they saw. They raised objections—fear of a strong central government, loss of state powers, apprehensions about a powerful chief executive and military, concerns about the dominance of the northern states—that would not disappear with ratification. In fact, southern criticisms of the political institutions and relationship founded by the Constitution would grow during the next century.

Most of the issues that would later tear the union apart were raised by Patrick Henry at the Virginia ratifying convention. He spoke with powerful eloquence and deep emotion about the threats to liberty and states' rights posed by the new political order. To each of his attacks, James Madison would respond with compelling analyses and cogent reasoning. Henry was ahead of his time. If the Constitution was founded on a solid foundation of reason, the experience of the coming decades would reveal that it would be ripped asunder by the passions of human emotions. Madison may well deserve the title of "Father of the Constitution." If so, it was Henry who sketched a rough draft of its obituary.

## CONCLUSION

The vows of union that were exchanged among the delegates of the several states in Philadelphia in 1787—and later reaffirmed in individual state ratifying conventions—sealed a strained if not unholy alliance. (When Alexander Hamilton was asked why there was no mention of God in the Constitution he replied, "We forgot.") Samuel Adams thought that the new nation had a blank sheet upon which to write, but the society had been writing its history for almost two hundred years and the sheet already had much scribbled upon it. What was done in Philadelphia that particularly hot and humid summer represented the first serious attempt at republican government in several hundred years, and amidst the collapse of totalitarian regimes today it is often noted in self-congratulatory tones that the American constitutional republic is the oldest in the world. And that is true, but it helps the image of an enduring republic if one conveniently forgets that the whole thing fell violently apart only a couple of generations later, and required the bloodiest war in the history of the Western Hemisphere—before or since—to put it back together again.

It was a strained union because it wedded two groups of multiple partners who long had followed different paths. The Northern colonies were animated by a commercial and acquisitive spirit based on free labor, a society of merchants and artisans and craftsmen and small farmers already industrializing. The South was claimed by a planter elite who would come to control an

**TABLE 3.2** Powers Denied to the States

1. States cannot enter into any treaty, alliance, or confederation.
2. States cannot coin money.
3. States cannot accept paper currency in payment of debts.
4. States cannot pass laws impairing the obligation of contracts.
5. States cannot tax imports or exports.
6. States cannot engage in war.

**TABLE 3.3** Powers Retained by the States—By Area

1. Regulation of property (including slavery).
2. Estate and inheritance law.
3. Banking and insurance.
4. Local government.
5. Criminal procedures, punishment, penal codes, sentencing.
6. Prisons.
7. Education.
8. Police powers.
9. Regulation of professions and occupations.
10. Zoning and land use.
11. Regulation of water, minerals, and natural resources.
12. Voting, elections, and political parties.
13. Family, business and consumer law.
14. Adjudication of most civil disputes.
15. Provision of basic services such as health, welfare, police and fire protection, transportation, recreation, and sanitation.

economic and political system based on the labor of African slaves, a society steeped in aristocratic traditions and pretensions and patterned on distorted images of ancient republican glories. Slavery would prove to be the greatest miscalculation of the constitutional framers. It, more than any other issue, would provide fertile ground for enormous amounts of wishful thinking as well as political mischief. The Union created in the summer of 1787 would not survive it.

## RECOMMENDED READINGS

Banning, Lance. 1985. "From Confederation to Convention: The Revolutionary Context of the Great Convention." *This Constitution, 6* (Spring): 12–18.

Beard, Charles A. 1913. *An Economic Interpretation of the Constitution of the United States.* New York: Macmillan.

Jillson, Calvin and Cecil L. Eubanks. 1984. "The Political Structure of Constitution Making: The Federal Convention of 1787." *American Political Science Review, 28* (August).

Parenti, Michael. 1980. "The Constitution as an Elitist Document," in Robert A. Goldwin and William A. Schambra (Eds.), *How Democratic is the Constitution?* Washington, DC: American Enterprise Institute for Public Policy Research.

Smith, David G. 1985. *The Convention and the Constitution: The Political Ideas of the Founding Fathers.* New York: St. Martin's Press.

Wood, Gordon S. 1969. *The Creation of the American Republic: 1776–1787.* Chapel Hill: University of North Carolina Press.

Wood, Gordon S. 1987. *The Making of the Constitution.* Waco, TX: Baylor University Press.

# 4

# *Federalism*

Change and Federalism

Federal Systems
*The Advantages of Federalism*
*Disadvantages of Federalism*

State and National Powers
*Court Decisions*
*Amendments*
*Money*

Stages of Federalism

Challenges to Federalism

The Ultimate Challenge

The Future of Federalism

---

Republican leaders are correct in attempting to give back to states and localities custody over basic public services and other programs that foster economic development. When control over these policies is decentralized to state and local governments, the country enjoys a more efficient and productive public sector. But Democratic leaders who defend national direction of social programs are correct in concluding that redistributive policy is the job of the national government. The very competition among states and localities that enhances local capacity to facilitate economic development destroys their ability to fund high-quality social programs. Any state that provides effective programs for the needy becomes a welfare magnet that attracts more poor people from other parts of the country. To avoid becoming a magnet, each state is forced to cut its welfare benefits, inducing among the states a race to the bottom.

—Paul Peterson *The Price of Federalism*

## CHANGE AND FEDERALISM

The precise contours of the emerging federal system cannot yet be perceived. However, we can suggest several factors that are likely to give it identifiable shape. First, the states will be forced to assume a greater share of the burden of governing as the national government continues to shed both financial and functional responsibility for programs and services. Second, suburban and other local governments will continue to grow in power and importance. This decentralization of political authority in the nation will enhance the likelihood of several long-run developments. For example, states—and particularly suburban governments—will exhibit little enthusiasm for the variety of costly social welfare programs that the national government has traditionally provided. In addition, states and localities will be limited in their assumption of new program responsibilities by the need to balance their budgets. Further, state and local governments have typically relied upon regressive taxes (those that impose a heavier tax burden on lower income families) such as sales and property taxes to generate revenues. Consequently, the growing revenue needs of these governments will, in the long-run, translate into a further redistribution of the tax burden between the rich and poor.

Finally, it is probable that the gradual shift of political power and responsibility from the national government to the states will be accompanied by an equally steady shift in the focus and purpose of government. Unlike the national government, the states will be less inclined to champion the interests of consumers, minorities, the disadvantaged, and the needy. They will be more likely to emphasize basic services and functions, such as transportation, police protection, education, and the criminal justice system.

But the shift in political power from the national government to states and localities will entail more than a systematic bias against higher taxes and social welfare programs. It will also initiate an era of more exclusive government. Suburban jurisdictions are inclined to pursue narrow, self-interested solutions to policy problems. With the decline of national authority and responsibility, the danger exists that efforts at shaping national solutions to problems that afflict the country as a whole will be abandoned in favor of more parochial approaches. Local and regional interests—rather than the national interest—will be more likely to prevail in the new federal system.

## FEDERAL SYSTEMS

The United States is among the relative handful of countries in the world that have a federal rather than a unitary political system. In a *unitary system,* a single central government controls and exercises political power and authority. In a *federal system,* two or more units of government exercise power and jurisdiction over the same geographic area and population. Although a unitary system may provide for regional and local units of government, these subunits are generally weak and are subject to the ultimate authority of the central government. In a federal system, however, each level of government exercises distinct and exclusive powers in specified areas. These powers are assigned and guaranteed by a constitution. Citizens in a federal system enjoy, in effect, dual citizenship. There are less than two dozen federal political systems in the international arena today.

Federal systems tend to be found in those nations with significant political, ethnic, social, and cultural divisions. When these differences coincide with geographical regions, a federal system is even more likely to be adopted. The early development of American society was conducive to federalism since the individual colonies were largely autonomous and pursued separate paths. Differences also crystallized on the basis of political values and ideology. The northern states developed a more democratic and egalitarian political culture, while the southern states exhibited an elitist and traditional approach to political issues. The states were also different economically. The South was dominated by an agricultural economy, while the North developed a powerful industrial and manufacturing sector. Finally, slavery would prove to be a particularly divisive issue among the states.

## The Advantages of Federalism

Federal systems are alleged to have several advantages. First, the individual states are allowed considerable discretion and flexibility in terms of adopting and implementing their own policy responses to political problems. No single and uniform set of national laws are unwillingly forced upon the entire

New York State Assembly in session. (Credit: Alan Carey/The Image Works)

population. Instead, each state enjoys a great deal of freedom with respect to the types of educational, penal, police, environmental, and welfare policies it will pursue. Some states choose to spend a great deal of money for public education and social welfare programs, while others spend relatively little. Some emphasize a major role for state and local governments in terms of aggressively coping with a variety of social and economic problems, while other states minimize governmental activity and encourage private sector solutions. According to this argument, therefore, federalism diffuses conflict in ethnically, racially, and politically diverse communities by allowing different groups to fashion their own policy solutions to perceived problems. Environmentally sensitive citizens in Oregon, Mormons in Utah, wealthy suburbanites in Connecticut, and fundamentalist Baptists in Texas have significant opportunities to enact the types of legislation they choose. This so-called freedom of choice—while certainly not unlimited—does provide individual states and communities with much more governmental discretion than would be available in a unitary system.

Another advantage of federalism is that it provides multiple points of access for individuals and groups pursuing a redress of grievances. If a group is denied a favorable response to its political demands at the national level, it has the option of seeking a successful resolution at the state and local levels. Political defeat at one level in a federal system is never final. Numerous opportunities exist for groups and individuals to press their political demands at a variety of other junctures. Legislatures exist at the national, state, and local levels. Courts operate nationally and locally as well as in state governments. Executives and bureaucrats implement and administer laws and programs at all levels of the political system.

Yet another advantage of federalism is that it may make the delivery of services and programs more manageable, more efficient, and more responsive. According to this perspective, the best government is the one closest to the people. Therefore, education, police and fire protection, social welfare, refuse collection, and recreation services can best be provided if they are delivered by local units of government. Only these community-level governments can effectively respond to the immense variation in local needs, preferences, and demands for services and programs. This argument holds that if a single unitary government attempted to administer basic services for the entire nation, a monstrously inefficient and singularly unresponsive service delivery bureaucracy would be the inevitable by-product.

Innovation in governmental activities is also supposedly enhanced by federalism. This interpretation holds that the thousands of state and local governments constitute a massive political laboratory, an experimental environment in which new and different public sector programs, services, and initiatives are constantly being adopted, proposed, implemented, tested, revised, and evaluated. These innovations take place in the public schools, in prisons, in police and fire departments, in welfare bureaucracies, and in transportation systems. Some of the programs initiate changes in auditing, accounting, and evaluation practices, other innovations occur in personnel management, computer technology, inmate rehabilitation, traffic engineering, and crime-fighting strategies, while still others undertake changes in teacher training and performance and fiscal administration. Of the thousands of innovations that are implemented on an annual basis throughout the nation, many are rejected as failures and discarded. Others, however, are evaluated as successes and adopted as permanent features of government. These effective innovations are then publicized and incorporated by other state and local governments.[1] In fact, many innovations are eventually copied by the national government as well. Within a federal system, there appears to be a great deal of opportunity for the thousands of different and independent units of government to create, to experiment, and to propose and adopt novel programs in an effort to solve problems. Federalism is a dynamic rather than a static form of political organization.

A city council meeting in Austin, Texas. (Credit: Bob Daemmrich/The Image Works)

It is also maintained that federalism nurtures public support for the system and encourages political stability. Citizens have numerous opportunities to participate at the local, state, and national levels. They can vote in dozens of different elections, run for political office, lobby government officials, and join interest groups. Through their participation and involvement, citizens perceive that they have a stake and play a significant role in public affairs. This involvement in and identification with government contributes to the development of public support for the political system.

Finally, it is argued that federalism enhances and promotes the freedom of individual citizens. The multitude of different centers of political decision making at the national, state, and local levels ensures that no one level or branch of government will be able to establish domination over the others. Further, the wide array of access points available to those wishing to press their demands and grievances upon public authorities encourages the formation of

---

[1] Robert L. Savage, "Diffusion Research Traditions and the Spread of Policy Innovations in a Federal System," *Publius 15* (Fall: 1986).

numerous interest groups. These groups, in turn, compete with each other over the allocation of scarce resources. This constant process of conflict, bargaining, accommodation, and compromise ensures that no single group will ever be able to achieve hegemony over the others.

## Disadvantages of Federalism

One of the suggested advantages of federalism is that it diffuses conflict in diverse societies. However, the emphasis within federal systems upon the diffusion of conflict also represents a potential source of weakness. Why is federalism often the political arrangement of choice in diverse societies? The answer revolves around the fact that federalism represents a compromise. Diverse and conflicting groups would find it difficult to exist under a unitary system. Federalism allows them to retain very considerable independence and power. The southern states, for example, were permitted to retain ownership of slaves. American federalism also accepted other major differences among the various parties to the Constitution by joining a commercial, industrializing region with one dominated by agrarian interests and institutions. Further, the constitutional framework attempted to reconcile significant disagreements concerning the issues of states' rights, national power, and the sovereignty of the people.

However, the federal system did not *solve* these problems. It only delayed a resolution of the issues that divided the states. In fact, these differences were so profound that they could not be resolved short of a long and bitter Civil War. Although the Civil War provided a solution to some of the problems that had plagued the original federal system (slavery, for example), the states retained considerable power and authority. Some of them would use that power to delay and obstruct national policy goals. In 1954, for example, the Supreme Court held in *Brown v. Topeka Board of Education* that "separate but equal" public school facilities for black students violated the equal protection of the laws guarantee of the Fourteenth Amendment and were unconstitutional. In that decision, the Court ruled that desegregation of racially segregated public schools should occur with "all deliberate speed." However, the reaction to the decision—particularly in the southern states—was bitter. Southern officials raced to outdo each other in terms of the direness of their predictions. Doomsday scenarios ranged from predictions of widespread interracial marriages and the "mongrelization of the white race," to "the end of civilization as we know it." More important than the racist-laden rhetoric, however, was the resistance to the desegregation order in the South. In a unitary system, the governmental procedures, precedents, and machinery would be available to implement a national policy decision at the local level. In the American federal system, however, many national laws heavily depend on other levels and units of government for implementation. When such policy choices reflect a national consensus and coincide with prevailing public opinion and values, putting the law into effect is a relatively easy task to achieve. When the decision is a highly controversial one, however, lower levels of government have numerous opportunities to delay, obstruct, and even defeat the implementation of national policies.

The *Brown* desegregation ruling illustrates how unpopular national decisions can be resisted in a federal system. Public education is largely under the control of state governments. Although the national government exerts considerable influence through federal aid to education, it is the states that establish and administer curriculum, personnel, and funding policies. In turn, state governments delegate much of this power and authority to local units of government—primarily school districts and cities. In response to the Supreme Court's ruling in *Brown* to desegregate the public schools with "all deliberate speed," many southern school districts simply ignored it. Others proposed plans that were unrealistic or unworkable. Since the federal judiciary had very limited enforcement power, there was essentially nothing that it could do to ensure compliance. Even though desegregation of the public schools had been the "law of the land" since 1954, that law would be effectively resisted for decades.

There is only one national government in the federal system. However, there are 50 state governments, 3,000 county governments, 35,000 municipal and town governments, 15,000 school district governments, and 30,000 special district governments. Most national policies depend upon these more than 80,000 state and local governments for implementation. When they find a particular national decision distasteful, they can effectively frustrate the implementation of the national agenda. Even as late as 1981, the U.S. Commission on Civil Rights issued a report in which it found numerous violations of the rights of minority citizens to register and vote in the states of Alabama, Georgia, Louisiana, Mississippi, North Carolina, South Carolina, and Texas.[2] These violations occurred despite the fact that such behavior had been outlawed by the national Voting Rights Act of 1965, plus the 1970 and 1975 revisions and extensions of the law.

## STATE AND NATIONAL POWERS

Originally, Congress was granted only a limited set of powers and responsibilities under the Constitution. It had the authority to conduct internal improvements, levy tariffs, administer public lands, regulate the currency, and issue patents. While certainly not insignificant, these powers were dwarfed by those assigned to the states. State governments had responsibility for regulating property (including slavery); for estate and inheritance; for banking, credit,

---

[2] U.S. Commission on Civil Rights, *The Voting Rights Act: Unfulfilled Goals.* Washington, DC: U.S. Commission on Civil Rights.

and insurance; for all units of local government including towns, cities, counties, and special districts; for criminal procedures and punishment, penal codes, prisons, and police protection; for laws regulating professions and occupations; and for the regulation of land use, water, and minerals. In addition, states were responsible for voting, elections, and political parties; for family, business, and consumer law; for the enforcement of most criminal laws and the adjudication of most civil disputes; and for the provision of basic services including health, education, and welfare. Further, the Tenth Amendment stipulates that "The powers not delegated to the United States by the Constitution, nor prohibited by it to the states, are reserved to the States respectively, or to the people." The national government is given a very specific and limited set of powers. All others belong to the states. In fact, however, the national government has been the senior partner in the federal relationship throughout much of American history. What developments accounted for the erosion of the states as once equal or even dominant partners in the federal arrangement? Three factors have been prominent: Supreme Court decisions, constitutional amendments, and money.

## Court Decisions

The Constitution is silent on the issue of who will interpret its meaning in those instances where there are conflicting interpretations as to what the words imply. Enter *Marbury v. Madison.* In 1800, Thomas Jefferson, a Democratic-Republican, was elected president. The incumbent, John Adams—a Federalist—engaged in a last minute rush to fill vacant positions in the judiciary with Federalist appointees. For example, during his last few weeks in office, Adams appointed John Marshall—his former Secretary of State—as Chief Justice of the Supreme Court. On his last night as president, Mr. Adams stayed up late signing commissions to office. One of these commissions was for a William Marbury to be a justice of the peace. The Commission, however, wasn't delivered before President Adams left office. It was now up to the new Secretary of State in the Jefferson Administration—James Madison—to do so. President Jefferson and Secretary Madison refused. In retaliation, Marbury sued Madison.

In a famous decision handed down by the Supreme Court under the new leadership of Chief Justice Marshall, the Court held that Secretary Madison should, in fact, have delivered the commission to Mr. Marbury. Of much more significance, however, was Marshall's additional ruling that the Judiciary Act of 1789 enacted by the Congress—and the law under which Marbury had brought his suit in the first place—was unconstitutional. Therefore, Marbury's claim was rejected because the law under which he had initially brought his suit was null and void. *Marbury v. Madison* is one of the most significant decisions in the history of American politics because it powerfully set the precedent of judicial review—the right of the Supreme Court to serve as the final arbiter of what the Constitution means. According to Chief Justice John Marshall, "An act of the legislature repugnant to the Constitution is void, and it is emphatically the province of the judicial department to say what the law is."

In *Marbury v. Madison,* the Federalists—who favored a strong central government—lost a skirmish but scored an important victory in the larger war. Although they were denied a minor judicial post, the decision to assign interpretative powers to the Supreme Court would come to represent a major coup for the Federalists. A branch of the national government now enjoyed the authority to give final meaning to the national Constitution. In *McCulloch v. Maryland,* that same Court would use that power to significantly strengthen the powers of the national government at the expense of the states.

In 1791, Congress had created a national bank with the authority to make loans and issue currency. The bank quickly became a major point of contention between those who wanted a strong central government, and the bank's opponents who viewed it as an infringement upon the constitutionally granted powers of the states. The issue came to a constitutional head in 1818 when the state of Maryland levied a tax on the Baltimore branch of the national bank. When bank officials refused to pay the tax, the state sued one of them—James McCulloch. After the state of Maryland won the first round in state court, the national government appealed the case to the Supreme Court. The state maintained that the Congress simply lacked the power under the Constitution to establish a national bank. According to Article I, Section 8, Congress was limited to powers that included borrowing and coining money, regulating commerce, creating judicial tribunals inferior to the Supreme Court, declaring war, raising and supporting an army and navy, and calling forth the militia. There was no mention of the power to create a national bank. However, the national government argued that in addition to its "enumerated powers," Congress also enjoyed "implied powers" under the "necessary and proper clause." The last part of Section 8 reads: "To make all Laws which shall be necessary and proper for carrying into execution the foregoing powers, and all other powers vested by this constitution in the government of the United States."

According to the national government, it was obvious that the framers intended to provide the Congress with the flexibility and discretion essential to an effective exercise of its enumerated powers. If Congress had the power to borrow and coin money, then certainly it also possessed the power under the necessary and proper clause to establish and operate a national bank as the appropriate instrument and mechanism whereby those specified powers could be put into effect. *McCulloch v. Maryland* was a crucial case in the early development of the federal system. If the states got their way, a narrow interpretation would be given to congressional power. Essentially, Congress would be limited to those specific powers enumerated in the Constitution. Such a strict interpretation, in conjunction with the Tenth Amendment stipulation that the powers not delegated to the national government or prohibited to the states belonged to the states or the people, would ensure a dominant role for the states in the federal system. But if the national government got its way, the Supreme Court would dramatically expand the specified powers of the Congress by giving a broad interpretation to the necessary and proper clause. The future of federalism, and the evolutionary development of the balance of power between the states and national government, hung on the outcome.

John Marshall and the Court struck a powerful blow against the power of the states in their ruling. In the decision in *McCulloch v. Maryland,* the justices held that national laws were supreme to state laws—the national supremacy doctrine. Further, they gave a broad interpretation to the necessary and proper clause, and thereby dramatically strengthened the powers of Congress. According to the Court, Congress enjoyed implied as well as enumerated powers under the Constitution. Five years later in *Gibbons v. Ogden,* the Supreme Court also gave Congress very broad power to regulate interstate commerce. These interpretations of national supremacy, necessary and proper, and interstate commerce, had a major impact in terms of enhancing the power of the national government at the expense of the states.

## Amendments

Two amendments added after the Civil War would further weaken the role of the states in the federal system. The Thirteenth Amendment had a direct and immediate effect by abolishing slavery in the states. The impact of the Fourteenth Amendment upon state power would not be felt for a full century, but when its influence was finally exerted, it would alter the relationship between the states and the national government. The Fourteenth Amendment would prove to be extremely significant because of its relationship to the Bill of Rights. To understand that complex relationship, we need to examine the issue of whether state governments were originally limited by the prohibitions and limitations contained in the Bill of Rights. This issue was initially decided in 1833 in the case *Barron v. Baltimore.* The city of Baltimore had, in the process of paving various streets, dumped debris in the ocean near a wharf owned by Mr. Barron. He alleged that his business had been destroyed in the process. In court, Barron argued that the city had taken his property (by destroying it) in violation of the Fifth Amendment of the Bill of Rights. According to the Fifth, "No person shall be deprived of life, liberty, or property, without due process of law; nor shall private property be taken for public use without just compensation." To Barron, the situation was clear-cut; the government had deprived him of his property without due process and had taken his private property without just compensation. The Supreme Court, however, held against him. The majority opinion concluded that,

> The Constitution was ordained and established by the people of the United States for themselves, for their own government, and not for the government of the individual states. Each state established a constitution for itself and in that

constitution provided such limitations and restrictions on the powers of its particular government as its judgment dictated. . . . The fifth amendment must be understood as restraining the power of the general government not as applicable to the States.

In essence, the Supreme Court held in *Barron v. Baltimore* that the Bill of Rights did not apply to the states. If a citizen were deprived by the state government of a constitutional protection guaranteed under the Bill of Rights, relief could not be sought from the national government. *Barron v. Baltimore* affirmed the concept of dual citizenship. Citizens were citizens of both the United States and their respective states, and the Bill of Rights extended its constitutional guarantees only to the former, and not the latter category. The Fourteenth Amendment was almost certainly adopted to broaden the extent of the coverage of constitutional protections to include citizens of the several states. The language of the Amendment appears to express that intent: "No state shall make or enforce any law which shall abridge the privileges or immunities of citizens of the United States, nor shall any state deprive any person of life, liberty, or property, without due process of law." However, the Supreme Court ignored the Fourteenth Amendment for several decades. Finally, it began to nationalize or "incorporate" the Bill of Rights into the Fourteenth. Table 4.1 presents the chronology of incorporation for the various constitutional protections contained in the Bill of Rights.[3]

The process of extending the Bill of Rights to restrict the activities of state governments as well as the national government has seriously eroded the ability of the states to control the behavior of their citizens. The states today exercise much less power than they once did under the federal system in areas such as criminal procedure, capital punishment, abortions, the rights of criminal suspects, and the authority to legislate restrictions regarding the freedoms of speech, press, and assembly.

## Money

Although judicial decisions and constitutional amendments have seriously weakened the status of the states in the federal system, no factor in recent decades has made a greater contribution to the further erosion of their constitutional standing than money. The states have needed money and the national government has provided them with huge amounts of it. As we can see in Table 4.2, federal grants to state and local governments increased from only $2 billion in 1950 to $137 billion in 1990. Almost one out of every five dollars spent by state and local governments today are provided by federal

---

[3] Richard C. Cortner, *The Supreme Court and the Second Bill of Rights: The Fourteenth Amendment and the Nationalization of Civil Liberties* (Madison: University of Wisconsin Press, 1981).

**TABLE 4.1** Incorporation of Bill of Rights Freedoms by Supreme Court Decision

| Freedom | Court Case | Year |
|---|---|---|
| Freedom of Speech | *Gitlow v. New York* | 1925 |
| Freedom of Press | *Near v. Minnesota* | 1931 |
| Freedom of Assembly | *Hague v. CIO* | 1939 |
| Freedom from Unlawful Search and Seizure | *Mapp v. Ohio* | 1961 |
| Right to Counsel in a Criminal Trial | *Gideon v. Wainwright* | 1963 |
| Right Against Self-Incrimination and Forced Confessions | *Escobedo v. Illinois* | 1964 |
| Right to Counsel and to Remain Silent | *Miranda v. Arizona* | 1966 |
| Right to Privacy | *Roe v. Wade* | 1973 |

grants. With federal money came federal influence. The old adage that there is no such thing as a free lunch has certainly been the case with federal dollars. It has been through the financial aid program that the national government has been able to force state governments to do what it could not make them do under the Constitution. Before we examine the causes and consequences of federal grants-in-aid, we need to trace the historical evolution of the federal system.

## STAGES OF FEDERALISM

Between 1789 and 1932 a system known as *dual federalism* prevailed. The states and national government each exercised separate and well-defined powers. It was the states rather than the national government that most aggressively dealt with domestic problems such as meat packing, food processing, working conditions and the regulation of child labor, railroads, and utilities. The national budget was small and national responsibilities were limited. The Great Depression that began in 1932 inaugurated a new era in the national-state relationship known as *cooperative federalism.* This stage in the historical evolution

**TABLE 4.2** Federal Aid to State and Local Governments

| | Federal Grants to State and Local Governments (in Billions) | As a Percentage of State and Local Government Expenditures |
|---|---|---|
| 1950 | $ 2.3 | 10.4% |
| 1960 | 7.0 | 14.7 |
| 1970 | 24.1 | 19.2 |
| 1980 | 91.5 | 25.8 |
| 1990 | 136.9 | 18.0 |

Source: U.S. Office of Management and Budget. *Budget of the United States Government: Fiscal Year 1995 Analytical Perspectives* (Washington, DC: U.S. Office of Management and Budget, 1994).

of the system lasted until 1960 and witnessed a spectacular burst of innovation and activity at the national level. The federal government undertook a broad array of regulatory initiatives and responsibilities in areas such as monetary policy, banking, the stock market, and the economy. The national government also joined with the states in a variety of programs. Significantly, however, the emphasis was upon cooperation rather than coercion. Although the national government provided most of the funding and devised program rules and regulations, it did not force controversial policies and programs upon the states. Instead, the partnership between the national and state governments was limited to policy areas where broad agreement, and even consensus with respect to the need for cooperative action, already existed. Even as late as 1960, three out of every four federal aid dollars were spent on only four programs—highways, old age assistance, aid to families with dependent children, and employment security. It is important to note, however, that while the national government did not coerce the states, it did engage in cooperative ventures with them in policy areas that previously had been the exclusive domain of the states. The national government now had its powerful foot in the door. During the next stage, it would kick that door open.

With *cooptive federalism* (1960–1980), the national government rejected cooperation in favor of setting and pursuing a national agenda.[4] Washington was no longer interested in simply helping the states achieve *their* goals. It was determined, instead, to accomplish its own policy objectives. To that end, the level of federal aid increased from 10 percent of state and local expenditures in 1950, to 19 percent in 1970, and 26 percent in 1980. In dollar amounts, federal aid totaled only $2.3 billion in 1950. By 1970, that figure had increased to $24 billion, and had further jumped to $91.5 billion by 1980. During cooptive federalism, the national government assumed responsibility for a variety of services that traditionally had been the responsibility of the states. Prior to the Depression, the only social welfare programs heavily funded by the national government were those designed to serve the needs of veterans. It provided no funding for public aid and housing, and federal expenditures accounted for only 12 percent of the spending for health and medical programs. By 1980, however, federal funding accounted for 68 percent of all expenditures for public aid programs, 92 percent of all spending for public housing, and 47 percent of the money spent for health and medical programs.

During the cooptive era of federalism, state and local governments grew increasingly dependent on the generous federal aid budget. However, the federal monies came with a complex set of strings attached. As a condition for successful receipt of federal aid, state and local governments were required to

---

[4] David B. Walker, "American Federalism Then and Now," pp. 23–29 in *The Book of the States, 1982–83* (Lexington, KY: Council of State Governments, 1982).

**TABLE 4.3**  National Laws That Increased Federal Power over the States

1. Civil Rights Act of 1964   Prohibited racial discrimination in public accommodations—hotels, motels, restaurants—and in employment.
2. Voting Rights Act of 1965   Outlawed literacy tests as a condition of voting; established penalties for interfering with the efforts of federal officials to register black voters.
3. Highway Beautification Act of 1965   Controlled advertising along major highways.
4. National Historic Preservation Act   Protected sites and buildings of historical, archaeological, and cultural significance.
5. Civil Rights Act of 1968   Prohibited racial discrimination in the sale and rental of housing.
6. Architectural Barriers Act of 1968   Ensured that buildings and facilities that are federally funded are accessible to the physically handicapped.
7. Clean Air Act of 1970   Set national emission and air quality standards.
8. Occupational Safety and Health Act of 1970   Provided for regulation of the workplace to ensure safe and healthy working conditions.
9. Educational Amendments of 1972   Prohibited discrimination in federally funded educational programs on the basis of sex.
10. Equal Employment Opportunity Act of 1972   Prohibited discrimination in employment in state and local governments.
11. Insecticide and Fungicide Act of 1972   Controlled pesticides that may be harmful to the environment.
12. Water Pollution Control Act of 1972   Established federal standards for the discharge of pollutants.
13. Rehabilitation Act of 1973   Prohibited discrimination against the mentally and physically handicapped in federally funded programs.
14. Resource Conservation and Recovery Act of 1976   Controlled hazardous wastes.
15. Surface Mining and Control Reclamation Act of 1977   Controlled surface mining.

comply with a variety of nationally imposed rules and regulations. As we can see in Table 4.3, Congress passed a number of laws during this period that extended federal influence in areas that traditionally had been the exclusive domain of the states. These laws prohibited discrimination in voting, housing, employment, public accommodations, and education. Other legislation established national standards for clean air and water, hazardous wastes, surface mining, insecticides, and health and safety in the workplace. During the era of cooptive federalism, the national government took the initiative and aggressively adopted new laws and programs to solve society's problems. It set national goals and priorities and heavily relied upon federal aid to coerce the states into accepting federal intervention in policy areas that previously had been reserved to the states.[5]

---

[5] James L. Sundquist, *Making Federalism Work* (Washington, DC: Brookings Institution, 1969).

Cooptive federalism fundamentally altered the federal system. For example, civil rights policy for racial minorities, women, and the physically handicapped was nationalized through a series of new laws and the antidiscrimination provisions attached to federally funded programs. Similarly, protection of the environment became a national responsibility. As late as 1948, it was congressional policy to "recognize, preserve, and protect the primary responsibilities and rights of the states in controlling water pollution." Today, however, it is the national government that has assumed primary responsibility for water and air pollution, solid waste management, chemical hazards, and environmental health and safety.[6]

A huge intergovernmental bureaucracy also developed to implement and administer the maze of new programs and services. These added layers of governmental machinery and employees had the effect of creating representative mechanisms for a number of groups that previously had little voice in political decision making: racial minorities, the poor, welfare recipients, the elderly, and the physically and mentally handicapped. As a result, the needs of these previously excluded groups in society were more effectively expressed, and their rights were better protected. The huge amounts of federal money that flowed down to states and localities during the era of cooptive federalism also had the effect of modernizing and professionalizing administrative structures at these levels. Police departments, for example, improved training, purchased new equipment and technologies, and innovated with respect to crime-fighting strategies. State and local bureaucracies responsible for social welfare, education, job training, health, working conditions, and environmental protection adopted new measures designed to improve everything from job performance and training to personnel and financial administration.

Another impact of cooptive federalism was that it established a basic, minimum level of services across the states. Federally funded welfare programs, for example, ensured that impoverished families with dependent children in all states would at least receive minimal monthly welfare payments. Even highly conservative states with a powerful tradition of rejecting public sector solutions to major statewide problems were prodded and even coerced by the national government into taking the first, halting steps to address these issues. For example, states that had long tolerated racial discrimination in education, employment, and voting were finally forced by the federal government to take action or lose federal funding.

The two decades of cooptive federalism (1960–1980) brought about some of the most rapid and profound changes in the history of the federal system,

---

[6] Advisory Commission on Intergovernmental Relations, *Protecting the Environment: Politics, Pollution, and Federal Policy* (Washington, DC: Advisory Commission on Intergovernmental Relations, 1981).

rivalled only by the abrupt and fundamental transformation of the federal arrangement as a result of the Civil War. During the era of cooptive federalism, the national government undertook a broad array of policy initiatives in areas ranging from welfare, education, crime, poverty, literacy, and urban renewal to civil rights, environmental protection, and worker safety. Washington was little interested in working within the existing federal structure on mutually agreed upon policies and programs that emphasized a high degree of consensus and cooperation. Instead, the national government established national goals and objectives, and pressured—even coerced the states—into a frequently reluctant acceptance. It was the closest the American Republic would come to a unitary system of government. If the trend toward usurpation by the national government of policy areas traditionally the exclusive province of the states had continued, it is probable that the federal system would have witnessed the most radical transformation of its structure and functions in the nation's history. Increasingly, the federal government would have set a national policy agenda, assumed a larger and larger share of state budget expenditures, and imposed an increasingly complex array of "strings" and conditions upon the receipt of federal aid. The nationalization of public policy would eventually have been achieved.[7]

However, the trend did not continue. Beginning in 1980, a series of developments suggested that the powerful surge toward cooptation of state power had run its course, and had even embarked upon a period of slow but steady decline. Several factors were responsible. First, a growing conservatism in the country—nurtured in part by widespread disenchantment with the federal programs of the 1960s and 1970s—culminated in the election of Ronald Reagan as president. Reagan introduced legislation that would have seriously eroded national cooptation of state power. However, a Democratic congress accepted only parts of the reform proposals. Considerable opposition to the Reagan initiatives came from the states themselves, who discovered that along with the throwing off of federal control would come a substantial loss of federal funding. The Reagan Administration did not, however, attempt to turn back the clock in all areas. For example, it supported the 55 mph speed limit on the nation's highways as well as a national minimum drinking age law—both had been enacted by the states under the threat of withdrawal of federal funding. Further, Reagan supported enhanced national power and jurisdiction in those policy areas that ranked high on the conservative social agenda, such as stronger federal enforcement powers for the war on drugs.

As Presidents Reagan and Bush appointed several conservative members to the Supreme Court, many observers expected that the Court would reverse

---

[7] Donald F. Kettle, *The Regulation of American Federalism* (Baton Rouge: Louisiana State University Press, 1983).

earlier decisions that enhanced national power at the expense of the states. While the justices have, in fact, chipped away at some of the landmark judicial decisions of cooptive federalism—such as *Roe v. Wade*—no consistent pattern has emerged. Sometimes the Court has sided with the states in constitutional disputes regarding the exercise of power within the federal framework. At other times, however, it has upheld the supremacy of national power.[8]

Another factor that brought the era of cooptive federalism to a close was the bankruptcy of the national government. Uncle Sam is broke, as well as hugely in debt. The reality of massive budget deficits provides little opportunity for increased levels of federal aid to the states. In fact, federal funding as a percentage of state and local government expenditures experienced a substantial decline between 1980 and 1990—from 26 percent to 18 percent. This drop dramatically reversed a steady increase in federal funding as a share of state and local expenditures—from 10 percent of state and local budgets in 1950, to 15 percent in 1960, 19 percent in 1970, and 26 percent in 1980.[9] Although the absolute dollar amount of federal aid has continued to grow, the proportionate annual increases have significantly slowed. For example, the level of federal funding to state and local governments grew by 300 percent between 1950 and 1960, by 343 percent between 1960 and 1970, and by 380 percent between 1970 and 1980. However, the rate of increase between 1980 and 1990 was less than 50 percent. The Gramm-Rudman-Hollings Deficit Control Act of 1985 has also had the effect of reducing the level of federal aid to the states.

The new emerging era in federalism—the latest stage in the evolutionary development of the American political system—is likely to represent on amalgamation of features from each of the earlier periods. In areas such as crime, drug enforcement, job training, and protection of minority rights, the nationalization of policy is likely to continue. In other areas, however, such as economic growth and education, the states will probably play a more aggressive and innovative role than the national government. In still other policy sectors—such as environmental protection—a cooperative approach between the two levels of government will likely prevail. In any event, the era that saw Washington set the domestic policy agenda for the entire country has ended. No longer will the national government engage in a cooptation of power and initiative in areas traditionally the exclusive domain of the states. The money is simply not available. Further, the public mood no longer supports the kind of widespread and aggressive use of public power to solve state and local problems that distinguished the period of cooptive federalism.

---

[8] Ann O. Bowman and Michael A. Pagano, "The State of American Federalism, 1989–1990," *Publius* 20 (Summer: 1990), pp. 1–27.
[9] U.S. Office of Management and Budget, *Budget of the United States Government: Fiscal Year 1995 Analytic Perspectives* (Washington, DC: U.S. Office of Management and Budget, 1994).

## CHALLENGES TO FEDERALISM

There have been periodic and substantial threats to the federal system. The first major challenge arose in 1812. Support for the decision to declare war on the British was regionally based, with the New England and Atlantic Coast states opposed to it. War fever was disproportionately concentrated in the southern and western states. There were a variety of motives for going to war. Some congressmen supported a declaration of war against the British because it would present an opportunity to take Florida from Spain—England's ally. Southern planters wanted control over the Florida Territory to deny a sanctuary to runaway slaves seeking refuge among the Seminole Indians. Others wanted war against the British to serve as a pretext for waging war against the Western Indian Confederacy. The Confederacy, which had long and bitterly resisted white settlement on its tribal lands, was allied with the British. Still others saw the war as a chance to take Canada from the British. Finally, "national honor" was at stake. President James Madison observed that "national honor is national property of the highest value."

An invasion of Canada was strongly opposed in the northeastern states. The governors of the New England states, in fact, refused to allow their militias to fight outside the borders of the United States. In Boston, merchants and bankers would not lend money to the national government, and individual citizens refused to buy war bonds. Congressman Daniel Webster from New Hampshire led the fight in Congress against the war by opposing the taxes and tariffs essential to the war effort. Citizen resistance to enlisting in the Army was widespread. Opposition to the war in this region was so strong that the Massachusetts legislature issued a call for a convention in 1814 "to lay the foundation for a radical reform of the National Compact." Representatives from all of the New England states attended the convention which was held in Hartford, Connecticut. Some, in fact, proposed secession, but majority sentiment advocated a revision of the national constitution. The delegates were particularly agitated about the domination of the presidency by the so-called "Virginia Dynasty." They proposed a constitutional amendment limiting the presidency to one term and rotating the office among different states. They further called for an amendment that would have required a two-thirds majority for both a congressional declaration of war and the admission of new states to the union.

The coming of peace with Britain diffused the opposition movement. However, the bitter division between the northeastern states on the one hand, and the southern and western states on the other over the issue of war, was indicative of the deep-seated strains and tensions in the federal system. The divisive issues that had been glossed over by the numerous compromises at the Constitutional Convention in 1787—slavery, states rights versus national power, merchants and industry versus planters and agriculture, the right of the people to govern themselves versus elitist fear of the tyranny of the majority—

still haunted the young republic. Constitutional compromise delayed the resolution of these problems. It could not solve them. In fact, the system of federalism itself represented a complex series of compromises among competing interests and conflicting ideas. The framers had pinned their hopes on devising the machinery of government in such a fashion that the compromise itself—the federal system—would be the solution. However, federalism simply transformed the way in which problems were dealt with. It could not solve the problems themselves. The issues of slavery and states' rights generated passions so intense that the federal system merely deferred a resolution rather than forced a solution.

Another challenge to the federal system came in 1832 when South Carolina adopted an "ordinance of nullification." The intent was to declare the national tariff acts of 1828 and 1832 null and void, and to prevent federal officials from collecting duties within the state. Led by John C. Calhoun, the proponents of nullification based their political arguments against the supremacy of national power on the Kentucky Resolution of 1798. That Resolution held that the national government was composed of a compact of states, and that "as in all other cases of compact among parties having no common judge, each party has an equal right to judge for itself." The South Carolinians argued that sovereignty rested with the people of each state. Only the "principals" acting through state constitutional conventions—similar to the conventions in the individual states that ratified the Constitution—could pass judgment on the constitutionality of laws enacted by Congress. Each state reserved the right to declare a law null and void. Unless three-fourths of the other states approved an amendment bestowing upon Congress the authority to pass the law at issue, the particular act would be null. Even if the requisite number of states passed the amendment in question, the dissenting state could secede from the union if it so decided. The nullification crisis provided the background for the famous exchange between President Andrew Jackson—an ardent Unionist—and Vice President John Calhoun. The occasion was a White House dinner in honor of Thomas Jefferson's birthday. President Jackson offered a toast to "Our Federal Union—it must be preserved." Calhoun countered with a toast of his own, "The Union—next to our liberty most dear. May we all remember that it can only be preserved by respecting the rights of the states and distributing equally the benefits and burdens of the Union."

The nullification crisis of 1832 never represented a serious threat to federalism and union. South Carolina's political isolation, in conjunction with President Jackson's strong opposition to nullification, ensured that the doctrine would come to naught. It should be emphasized, however, that less than 30 years later, South Carolina would follow through on her earlier threat, and secede from the Union. And this time she would be joined by ten of her sister states. It is important to consider the context in which the nullification crisis took place, for while the crisis itself would pass, the conditions that produced it would not. South Carolina in 1832 exhibited an intense insecurity about the huge number of slaves in the population. The planter elites lived in contrast fear of two things: a slave uprising, and efforts by the national government to interfere with the institution of slavery. They already had the example to contemplate of the British government in 1831 initiating a program of gradual emancipation of the slaves in the West Indies. The growing anti-slavery movement in the northern states also threatened to develop into a formidable political foe. Under the leadership of evangelical ministers, the abolitionists demanded immediate emancipation. One of their most influential leaders was William Lloyd Garrison who founded the New England Antislavery Society. His hatred of slavery was evidenced by the fact that years later he would publicly burn a copy of the Constitution and proclaim, "So perish all compromises with tyranny."

The abolitionists were experts at mass mailings. In 1835, they mailed out more than a million pieces of antislavery literature. The number of abolitionist societies grew from 200 in 1835 to 500 in 1836 and to 2,000 in 1840. They claimed a membership of 200,000 citizens. A major strategy employed was to flood the Congress with petitions demanding the elimination of the "three-fifths compromise" from the Constitution, the prohibition of the domestic slave trade, and the refusal to admit new slave states to the Union. By 1838, 500,000 signed petitions had already been delivered to public officials in Washington. It is little wonder, then, that the southern states had grown increasingly uneasy—even paranoid—over the direction of federalism and their role in the political system. Their confidence was further shaken by a slave rebellion in 1831. Led by Nat Turner, the rebellious slaves killed 60 slaveholders and family members in Virginia before they themselves were killed or captured. Whites retaliated by killing numerous blacks in the county, with one group of militiamen killing 40 blacks and staking the heads of 15 of them on poles. Turner was captured and hanged, along with 20 of his followers.

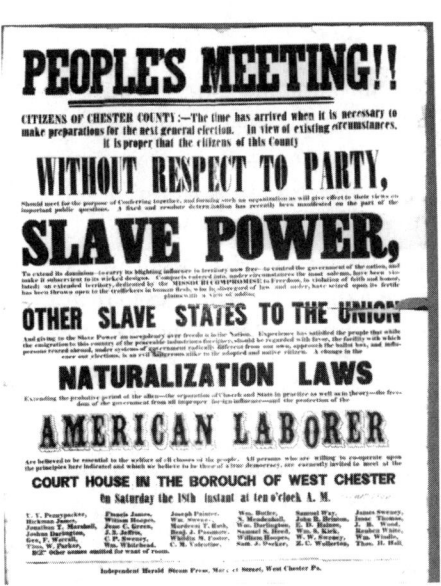

Advertisement for a public rally opposing slavery. (Source: American Antiquarian Society)

The Nat Turner Rebellion sent powerful tremors throughout the South. Shortly afterwards, the Virginia assembly rejected a proposal of gradual emancipation by a vote of 73 to 58. From that point on, the southern states increasingly turned inward. They began to devote enormous energy and attention to creating elaborate political and intellectual justifications for slavery. They also enacted laws that provided for even more severe control and discipline of the slave population. It is in this context that the nullification crisis should be understood. It represented a state challenge to the power of the national government, aggravated by a deep and growing concern over the issues of slavery, and the rights of the states within the federal system.

## THE ULTIMATE CHALLENGE

In retrospect, it can be seen that the constitutional contract creating the Union concealed enormous tensions and strains. A slave society was merged with one of free men; an industrializing economy engaged in partnership with an agricultural one; men who championed direct democracy and state supremacy entered into a political compact with elitists who espoused a strong central government run by virtuous gentlemen drawn from an aristocracy of talent. They had tried to compromise away their profound differences, but their unnatural alliance had finally come unhinged over "irreconcilable differences." When the eleven southern states seceded the federal system created by the Constitutional Convention in Philadelphia in 1787 had, for all intents and purposes, failed. Federalism had worked for only two generations and there would be no way to put the pieces back into workable condition short of the bloodiest war in the history of the Western Hemisphere.

As is the case with respect to other important issues, the Constitution is silent on the question of secession. Many southerners claimed that state sovereignty had come before national sovereignty, that by voluntarily joining the federal union they had delegated only some of the *functions* of sovereignty to the central government. Significantly, they had retained sovereignty itself. They further argued that just as individual state conventions had ratified the Constitution, so could individual state conventions decide to withdraw from it. Other Southerners maintained that while they did not have a constitutional right to secession, they did have a right to revolution. "Were not the men of 1776 secessionists?" asked one of them. They pointed to the Declaration of Independence and its words on the rights of men.

> That to secure these rights, Governments are instituted among men, deriving their just powers from the consent of the governed. That whenever any Form of Government becomes destructive of these ends, it is the Right of the People to alter or abolish it, and to institute new Government . . . when a long train of abuses and usurpations . . . evinces a design to reduce them under absolute Despotism, it is their right, it is their duty, to throw off such Government, and to provide new Guards for their future security.

Just as the original thirteen colonies had revolted against the despotism of the British King, so the eleven southern states were now revolting against the equally intolerable despotism of the national government. It took the Civil War to settle the issue. Before the Civil War, citizens referred to the Union as "The United States are . . ." It was not until after the war that they referred to the nation as "The United States is . . ."

## THE FUTURE OF FEDERALISM

Throughout the history of the nation, the federal system has undergone a period of change. Originally, the states and national government exercised power in separate and distinct spheres of public authority, with the states assuming a preponderance of responsibility for governing. This stage was eventually replaced by one that emphasized a cooperative relationship, followed by an era of national dominance within the federal framework. This letter stage has now also come to an end, to be replaced by one whose contours are still emerging. This latest period in the evolutionary development of American federalism combines elements of the previous three. The national government will retain jurisdiction in some areas (protection of minority rights), while state governments will dominate in others (education, economic development). In still other policy arenas, responsibility will be shared (environmental protection, welfare). Another important difference between the new era of federalism and past stages is that the current period is distinguished by a resurgence of state power. The national government has lost its momentum, hamstrung by budget deficits and the growing political conservatism of the electorate. State governments, on the other hand, have been invigorated by the increasing political clout of suburban jurisdictions, by the corresponding decline of national power, and by the belief on the part of a new breed of energetic public officials that policy solutions require state and local (rather than national) resources and initiatives.

## RECOMMENDED READINGS

Advisory Commission on Intergovernmental Relations. 1984. *Regulatory Federalism: Policy, Process, Impact, and Reform.* Washington, DC: Advisory Commission on Intergovernmental Relations.

Cortner, Richard C. 1981. *The Supreme Court and the Second Bill of Rights: The Fourteenth Amendment and the Nationalization of Civil Liberties.* Madison: University of Wisconsin Press.

Derthick, Martha. 1970. *The Influence of Federal Grants.* Cambridge, MA: Harvard University Press.

Elazar, Daniel J. 1984. *American Federalism: A View from the States.* New York: Harper & Row.

Kettle, Donald F. 1983. *The Regulation of American Federalism.* Baton Rouge: Louisiana State University Press.

Peterson, Paul, Barry Rabe, and Kenneth K. Wong. 1986. *When Federalism Works.* Washington, DC: Brookings Institution.

Sundquist, James L. 1969. *Making Federalism Work.* Washington, DC: Brookings Institution.

# 5

# *Interest Groups and Political Parties*

Change and Interest Groups
Change and the Party System
Interest Groups Gain Power
   *The Indians Win Again*
   *The Gospel According to Ralph*
The Functions of Interest Groups
Criticisms of Interest Groups
   *Labor as an Interest Group—A Case Study*
Resources
Public Perceptions of Interest Groups
Interest Group Tactics
   *Lobbying*
   *Efforts to Control Lobbyists*
   *Electioneering*
   *Public Relations Campaigns*
   *Protest Demonstrations*

*Women as an Interest Group—A Long and Winding Road*
*The Environment and Interest Groups*
*New Groups on the Block*
*Conclusion*
Political Parties
   *The Functions of Political Parties*
   *The Decline of Political Parties*
   *Party Identification*
   *Republican Growth*
   *Group Identification*
   *Ideological Unity*
   *Third Parties*
   *Party Organization*
   *A Decentralized Party System*
Conclusion

> There is an association, union, society, league, conference, institute, organization, federation, chamber, foundation, congress, order, brotherhood, company, corporation, bureau, mutual cooperative, committee, council, trusteeship, movement, assembly, club, board, or tribe for every human need, desire, motive, ambition, goal, aim, drive, affiliation, occupation, industry, interest, incentive, fear, anxiety, greed, compulsion, frustration, hate, reform, and cussedness in the United States.
>
> —James Deakin, *The Lobbyists*

## CHANGE AND INTEREST GROUPS

The changes described in Chapter 1 have already had a significant impact upon the nation's interest groups. These changes have led to the creation of new groups, have strengthened others, and weakened still others. Economic change has seriously eroded the strength and influence of some groups. Forty years ago, labor unions represented one-third of all American workers. Today, that proportion has declined to less than 15 percent. In the private sector, only one out of every ten workers belongs to a labor union. This membership decline has corresponded to an equally significant drop in the political influence of organized labor.

The population shift to the suburbs and the decline of inner-city neighborhoods has severely weakened those groups that have traditionally represented "big city" interests. Organizations that once articulated the demands of white ethnic neighborhoods, racial minorities, and the working class—such as Mayor Richard Daly's political machine in Chicago—no longer exist. "White flight" to the suburbs, in conjunction with cuts in federal spending for urban programs and services, have dramatically curtailed the political influence of those interest groups that speak for urban-based constituencies.

The "browning" of America has spawned a variety of new groups that are increasingly active with respect to racial issues. The aging of the population has also had a powerful impact on the changing interest group landscape. The largest interest group in the nation—with a membership of 33 million and a budget of several hundred million dollars—is the American Association of Retired Persons (AARP). One of the most influential interest groups in the country, it is expected that the AARP will continue to grow in numbers and political power as the population ages.

An increasingly elderly membership may, under certain conditions, operate to weaken a group's effectiveness. Veterans' organizations are a case in point. Although still a political force to be reckoned with (particularly with regard to veterans' health-care issues), the principal veterans organization—American Legion, Veterans of Foreign Wars (VFW), Disabled American Veterans—have suffered in recent years from declining memberships. World War I, World War II, Korea, and Vietnam generated a huge membership pool from which these organizations could draw. However, the abolition of a military draft, the absence of major foreign conflicts, and the end of the Cold War have combined to limit the current population of potential members and reduce their influence.

## CHANGE AND THE PARTY SYSTEM

The changes discussed in Chapter 1 have also had a significant impact on the political parties. The Republicans have been the major beneficiaries of these changes. For example, the population shift to the suburbs has worked to their advantage. Suburban residents are more conservative and are more inclined to vote Republican. The break-up of the once "Solid South" has also strengthened the Republicans. The typical Southern voter is now much more likely to vote for Republican candidates—and considerably less likely to cast a vote for the Democrats—than was the case only a few decades ago.

The decline of national power has also re-invigorated the Republican Party. The end of the era of "big government"—in conjunction with efforts to shift functional and financial responsibility for programs and services to the states—has also operated to the advantage of the Republicans. Having long opposed the growth of a powerful national government, the Republicans are now in a position to capitalize on the growing anti-government sentiment among the electorate. In a related vein, public concern and dissatisfaction with issues such as welfare, budget deficits, taxes, and crime has had the effect of identifying the Republicans as the party of fiscal conservatism, law and order, and "family values."

Sharon Pratt Dixon, Mayor of the District of Columbia, shows support at the 1992 Democratic National Convention. (Source: AP Photo)

The Democrats, on the other hand, have witnessed a steady erosion of their electoral base. In significant degree, their diminished popular support can be attributed to the forces of change. The transformation of the national economy, for example, has devastated the industrial sector. The resulting loss of manufacturing jobs, in turn, has severely weakened organized labor. The declining fortunes of organized labor has substantially weakened the Democrats' electoral coalition.

The population shift away from big cities has also hurt the Democrats. Once the party could rely on an alliance of big labor, big cities, and the "Solid South." Big city urban machines (such as Mayor Richard Daly's in Chicago), and mighty labor unions such as the AFL-CIO, could be consistently relied upon to turn out a massive vote for Democratic candidates. In combination with the electorally loyal southern states, this alliance proved to be a formidable one. Recent changes, however, have devastated the coalition. The growing Republican dominance in southern states, the decline of big cities, and the population shift to the suburbs have severely weakened the key constituencies of the Democratic Party. The challenge for the Democrats will be to build a new electoral alliance.

Native Americans celebrate the one-hundredth anniversary of the Battle of Wounded Knee. (Source: The Gamma Liason Network)

## INTEREST GROUPS GAIN POWER

New groups are constantly being formed. Some seek to achieve only limited political goals. Other interest groups are much more ambitious.

### The Indians Win Again

They have finally won a second victory at the Little Bighorn. As a result of recently enacted legislation sponsored by Senator Ben Nighthorse Campbell of Colorado—a Northern Cheyenne whose grandfather fought in the battle against General Custer—the name of the battlefield in Montana has been changed from Custer Battlefield to the Little Bighorn National Battlefield. It may seem like a small thing, but to members of the Black Hills Veterans Association—and to Native Americans in general—the name change represents a major symbolic victory. "Now I feel like I am welcome," observed Senator Campbell, "Indians have felt like second-class citizens. I tried to elevate the other side of the battle." The renaming of the site where George Armstrong Custer made his famous last stand in 1876 would never have happened without the lobbying efforts of various Native American interest groups.[1]

[1] *New York Times,* "Solemn Celebration Where Custer Fell," (November 11, 1993).

### The Gospel According to Ralph

Sometimes he does not even rest on Sundays. As executive director of the Christian Coalition, Ralph Reed is head of one of the most powerful interest groups in the country. Calling his organization "the McDonald's of American Politics," the Christian Coalition has 1,600 county chapters, claims 60,000 churches as members, relies on 1.6 million active supporters, and boasts a $25 million annual budget.[2]

Emerging as a significant political force in the 1970s under the leadership of Jerry Falwell and the Moral Majority, the "religious right" is today one of the most influential political movements in the nation. Building upon the vast mailing lists developed by Pat Robertson in his 1988 bid for the Republican presidential nomination, Ralph Reed has emphasized a grassroots approach in transforming the Christian Coalition into one of the most effective organizations in American politics. Committed to the idea that "The future of America is not shaped by who sits in the oval office but by who sits in the principal's office," the Christian Coalition conducts leadership schools where supporters are trained to establish "rapid-response networks" connected by phone, fax, and modem across the nation. This network can generate tens of thousands of calls and letters to lawmakers on any issue within a few hours.

The goal of the Christian Coalition is to eventually establish a cadre of at least 10 workers in each of the nation's 175,000 political precincts, a membership of 100,000 churches, and a budget of $50 to $100 million dollars. By mobilizing campaign workers and passing out 33 million voter guides (many in church pews) during the 1994 elections, the Christian Coalition is given credit by some observers for providing the winning vote margin for half of the Republicans' 52-seat gain in the House of Representatives. A survey conducted by *Campaigns and Elections Magazine* concluded that the religious right now exercises "considerable control" of Republican parties in 13 states and "completely dominates" in 18 others.

The Christian Coalition pursues a political agenda that emphasizes opposition to abortion and support of school prayer and welfare reform. Ralph Reed predicts an even more significant role for his organization. "If we do all that we can," he observes, "we will be larger and more effective and will reach more people than the Republican and Democratic parties combined."

## THE FUNCTIONS OF INTEREST GROUPS

Organized political groups represent every conceivable interest in society. Deriving their legitimacy from the First Amendment—which guarantees freedom of speech as well as the right to petition the government for a redress

---

[2] Jeffrey H. Birnbaum, "The Right Hand of God," *Time* (May 15, 1995), pp. 28–35.

of grievances—the employees of interest groups (lobbyists) seek to influence the decisions of countless bureaucratic agencies, regulatory commissions, White House officials, congressional committees, individual congressmen, and staffs. They exert enormous influence within the American political system. In this chapter, we will examine their functions, motives, organization, resources, tactics, and goals. We will also consider how the changes discussed in Chapter 1—demographic, social, economic, cultural, political—will impact the future role of interest groups. For all the criticisms of interest groups, they perform a series of vital functions that no other institution in society is capable of performing. For example:

- They represent people. By joining an interest group, citizens feel that their viewpoint and demands with respect to political issues are better represented than if they did not belong.
- They provide a solution to the intensity-of-preference problem. Citizens who feel strongly about a political issue—or set of political issues—can join an interest group and contribute their money and effort in support of the cause. Group membership and activity provides the opportunity for the continuous expression of intense preference in a way that the vote does not.
- They educate their members, the public, and political officials. Interest groups are often the first actors to call attention to problems in society. On issues ranging from environmental pollution and child abuse to abortion and gun control, they stimulate interest and attention through debate, research, lobbying, and publicity campaigns. For example, it was an interest group's reaction against a fashion statement that changed the way Americans see—and use—birds. In 1896, Harriet Lawrence Hemenway, a prominent Boston society woman and plumed hat wearer herself, read an article describing the devastation visited upon birds by feather hunters. Five million birds were slaughtered annually, with huge piles of skinned birds left to rot, the orphaned baby birds left to starve in their nests. The outraged Ms. Hemenway organized the Massachusetts' Audubon Society, eventually convincing a thousand other society matrons "to work to discourage the buying or wearing of feathers and to otherwise further the protection of native birds." By the 1920s, the Audubon Society had pressured both legislators and the public to make feathered fashion a thing of the past. Audubon Societies were quickly founded in other states, and in 1905 a national organization was founded. The National Audubon Society today has 570,000 members in 40 states. The national and state societies have taken the lead in promoting legislation to protect freshwater wetlands.
- They shape the public agenda. By dramatizing and publicizing political issues and problems, they structure and focus the national debate. Interest groups help establish priorities with respect to which problems and issues will receive top attention.
- They bring pressure to bear on public officials to take action in response to problems.

- They serve an oversight function. Interest groups act as watchdogs over public agencies, programs and officials.

## CRITICISMS OF INTEREST GROUPS

Some observers believe that interest groups represent a major flaw in the American political process. Specific criticisms include:

- Interest groups thwart the public will by obtaining special consideration and treatment of their narrow interests and demands.
- Interest groups are able to defy and deny the public interest by delaying, obstructing, and defeating legislation that enjoys broad, popular support.
- Interest groups corrupt the political process through the huge sums of money they spend during election campaigns to "buy" candidates for public office.
- In a system dominated by interest groups, a small number of wealthy people and corporations can spend a great deal of money and get their way. Under such an arrangement, the notion of popular will (as expressed through the outcome of elections) borders on the meaningless.
- Interest groups distort information, inflame passions, and play on people's biases and prejudices to get their way. National debate and reasoned analysis of policy alternatives are impossible in such an environment.

Interest groups are an inevitable byproduct of the manner in which the American political system is organized. James Madison, for example, sought a scheme of government in which "ambition would be pitted against ambition."[3] The separation of powers, the multiple branches of government, the network of checks and balances, and the system of shared powers under the federal framework, all encourage the proliferation of interest groups. Interest group activity represents an effort to marshall resources and concentrate power in a governmental system that was designed to fragment and decentralize political power.

### Labor as an Interest Group—A Case Study

As the first national labor union, the Noble Order of the Knights of Labor was started in 1869 as a secret society of Philadelphia garment cutters. It quickly shed its parochial nature, however, and sought to enlist workers across craft/occupational lines. The Knights of Labor even welcomed women and blacks as members. Offering an elaborate set of rituals and ceremonies that strongly appealed to the fraternal spirit of the nineteenth-century worker, the union quickly spread to other cities. By 1878, the Knights of Labor was a national movement. It would eventually claim 700,000 members. Employing the

---

[3] James Madison, *Federalist No. 10*.

boycott and the strike to achieve their demands, the Knights successfully concluded a strike against Jay Gould's Southwestern Railroad System in 1885. The movement would not endure, however. Seeking to address the social and economic evils produced by industrialization, the Knights of Labor pursued a broad-based reform agenda. They would eventually discover, however, that the average worker was more interested in short-term, economic gain than in a basic restructuring of society. As a result, rival unions such as the American Federation of Labor, organized along craft and trade lines and limiting their demands to wages and working conditions, would eventually displace the Knights of Labor.[4]

The last quarter of the nineteenth century would not be a good one for organized labor. Actively opposed by the political authorities and enjoying little support among the public at-large, unions would realize little progress. Efforts to improve wages and working conditions were resisted by business at every turn with the government acting as the corporate sector's willing ally. In 1877, for example, President Rutherford B. Hayes called out the National Guard to put down a series of labor strikes against the railroads. In 1886, the unions launched another wave of strikes against the railroads. After the death of four strikers during a battle between strikers and strike-breakers at the McCormick plant in Chicago, the organizers called a protest rally to be held at Haymarket Square. When the police attempted to disperse the gathering, a bomb was thrown and several policemen were killed. Although there was no evidence against them, four of the organizers were executed and others were sentenced to long prison terms.

The government continued its policy of employing force against the unions. In 1892, the Pennsylvania militia put down a strike by the Iron and Steel Workers Union against the Carnegie Steel Company. The following year, the workers at the Pullman Railroad Company (sleeping cars) went on strike when the owners cut wages but refused to lower the rent on company housing. In response to the widespread railroad strike that ensued, United States Attorney General Richard Olney—a former railroad lawyer—dispatched troops to keep the trains running. When the strike leaders refused to obey the injunctions issued against them, they were held in contempt of court and jailed. The strike was broken.[5]

The more radical the policies pursued by a particular union, the more extreme was the government's reaction. The Industrial Workers of the World (IWW) represent a case in point. Formed in 1905, the Wobblies (as they were

---

[4] Donald L. Kemmerer and Edward D. Wickersham, "Reasons for the Growth of the Knights of Labor in 1885–1886," *Industrial and Labor Relations Review, 3* (1950): 213–20.

[5] Gerald N. Grob, *Workers and Utopia: A Study if Ideological Conflict in the American Labor Movement* (Evanston, IL: Northwestern University Press, 1961).

known) were among the most militant of unionists. Hoping to eventually establish a workers' society, the IWW was strongest in the western states where it realized considerable success in organizing lumberjacks, construction workers, miners, and migrant farm workers. However, union leaders miscalculated the government's reaction when they spoke out against World War I and threatened to disrupt war production in the lumber and copper industries. The U.S. Justice Department promptly arrested 113 IWW officials for interfering with the war effort. Meanwhile, a mob in Butte, Montana, dragged IWW organizer Frank Little through the streets and hanged him from a railroad trestle. By the end of the war, the Wobblies had been driven out of existence.

The experience of labor unions demonstrates that the efforts of some interest groups to establish their political legitimacy may be strongly opposed by public authorities. The government's use of intimidation, legal tactics, federal troops, and even violence to retard the progress of organized labor testifies to that observation. However, labor's experience also illustrates that the intense concentration of numbers, effective organization, the marshalling of resources, and sustained political pressure over a long period of time can pay remarkable dividends. Eventually, government would relinquish the role of avowed enemy and cross over into labor's camp. In 1914, the Clayton Act—which recognized both the unions' right to organize and to strike—was enacted by Congress. During the Depression, the national government assumed the role of full-fledged ally. The National Labor Relations Act guaranteed the right of employees to join a union, prohibited employer practices such as the blacklisting of workers for participating in union activities, and upheld the right to collective bargaining. It also established the National Labor Relations Board to enforce these provisions. The Fair Labor Standards Act (1938) abolished child labor and created a minimum wage.

By the end of World War II, American labor had come full circle. From its origins as a radical outsider seeking a share of political and economic legitimacy, it had become a powerful and privileged member of the institutional elite. A three-way partnership between business, labor, and government had emerged. No longer engaged in a mutually antagonistic relationship, industry and government now accepted organized labor as a full partner in the economic and political business of the nation. Corporate leaders recognized the legitimacy of the unions, accorded them a major role in the collective bargaining arrangement, guaranteed jobs, and provided rank-and-file members with steadily rising wages and benefits. In return, the unions ensured a relatively stable workforce, and limited their demands to issues such as wages, hours, benefits, job classifications, and rules. The government pursued policies to guarantee predictability, rationality, and stability in the marketplace through agencies such as the Federal Reserve Board, the Departments of Commerce and Labor, and a variety of federal regulatory commissions.

It was a remarkable accomplishment. The partnership between business, labor, and government could take credit for the creation of a huge middle class, for a steady rise in the standard of living, for high employment, and for impressive and consistent levels of corporate profit.

Ironically, however, organized labor has once again fallen on hard times. Union membership as a proportion of the workforce is at a lower level than at any time since 1905. Foreign competition, automation, and the decline of the manufacturing sector have devastated organized labor's influence in the workplace as well as in the political arena. Strikes are unlikely to have a positive impact in an era of high unemployment. Union militancy is unlikely to bear fruit when the response of corporate officials is a threat to export more jobs overseas or even to close a plant down completely. The dramatic decline in the power of organized labor is testified to by the fact that despite stagnating and even declining wages, reduced benefits, abolition of job security, widespread job losses, and corporate firings, the current level and intensity of labor strikes are much lower than in decades past. Despite huge corporate profits and productivity gains of 2 percent a year, increases in workers' wages have been minimal.[6] Profits are used to build cash reserves, to further automate production, to finance corporate takeovers, and to compensate high-level executives—rather than to raise employee wages.

Recently, however, organized labor has shown signs of renewed vigor. John Sweeney, the newly elected head of the AFL-CIO (which represents 78 unions and 13 million members) promised to take labor down a more militant path. Observing that union members are treated "like so much road kill on the highway of American life," Sweeney announced that "America needs a raise." He vowed to revitalize the labor movement by training a thousand new organizers a year, spending 30 percent of the budget on organizational drives, and making a special effort to recruit women (women are consistently more pro-union than men) and minorities. Major emphasis will be given to organizing service employees such as janitors, hotel maids, and home-healthcare workers. During his tenure as head of the Service Employees International Union, Sweeney succeeded in doubling the union membership to more than a million.

Recent union mergers also indicate a renewed sense of urgency and purpose within this once powerful interest group. For example, the United Steelworkers have merged with the United Rubber Workers. In addition, the United Steelworkers, the United Automobile Workers, and the International Association of Machinists and Aerospace Workers will combine to form a two-million-member superunion. Success, however, will be difficult to achieve. A few decades ago, industrial workers accounted for 40 percent of the workforce. Today, they comprise less than one-fifth of the labor force. Membership in the

---

[6] Kevin Phillips, *The Politics of Rich and Poor* (New York: Random House, 1990).

United Automobile Workers, for example, has dropped from 1.5 million in 1979 to 800,000, while the number of workers belonging to the United Steelworkers has fallen from 380,000 to only 140,000.[7]

## RESOURCES

Interest groups are not created equal. Some are much more effective than others. Many factors influence the extent to which a particular group will accomplish a set of political goals. We will discuss a few of these factors.

*Group leadership* is a key element in determining interest group performance. For example, Ralph Nader is credited with energizing the consumer protection movement through his founding and leadership of the Center for Study of Responsive Law and Public Citizen. Similarly, many of the problems recently experienced by the National Association for the Advancement of Colored People (NAACP)—the nation's oldest civil rights organization—have been blamed on the past executive director, Benjamin F. Chaves, Jr. Hopes for re-vitalizing the NAACP center directly upon the new head, Kweisi Mfume, a former congressman and past leader of the Black Congressional Caucus.

*Size of membership* is also an important factor. Groups of only a few hundred or even a few thousand members are unlikely to have the impact necessary to influence policy outcomes. All other things being equal, a group such as the American Association of Retired Persons with 33 million members is likely to be more influential than an organization such as the National Association for the Advancement of Colored People (NAACP) with only 345 thousand members.

All other things are seldom equal, however. The American Medical Association (AMA) with only 300 thousand members is often more influential with respect to policy issues (healthcare reform, for example) than the AFL-CIO which claims a membership of 13 million. Why? One factor is the composition of the membership. Medical doctors are highly educated and well-paid. They enjoy high levels of both occupational prestige and public trust. Acknowledged experts in an extraordinarily complex field, they are sometimes the difference between life and death. It is little wonder then that their opinions and judgments concerning relevant policy matters are accorded considerable respect by political authorities. Labor union members, on the other hand, cannot compete in terms of education, income, occupational status, and expertise. With respect to many policy issues, the sheer weight of numbers provides a misleading indicator of interest group effectiveness.

---

[7] Peter T. Kilborn, "Why Labor Wants the Tired and Poor," (*New York Times,* October 29, 1995); and Peter T. Kilborn, "Delegates of Labor Gather, Battered But Now Buoyant," (*New York Times,* October 21, 1995).

*Money* is of crucial importance. In fact, money can overcome a number of obstacles. It can buy effective leaders. It can also compensate for a small membership. One of the reasons that the American Medical Association is such an effective interest group is that it commands enormous monetary resources. An examination of Table 5.1 reveals that its annual budget of $205 million ranks it only behind the American Association of Retired Persons (with annual expenditures of $305 million). Similarly, the Tobacco Institute makes up for its small membership (it represents 13 tobacco companies) with expenditures of $38 million a year, while the Sierra Club with only 650 thousand members spends $39 million annually.

The ideal situation for an interest group is to have both a large membership and a large budget. Two interest groups easily qualify. The largest in the nation in terms of both membership and money (with 33 million members and $305 million, respectively) is the American Association of Retired Persons. As the population continues to age, it is probable that both the size and the annual expenditures of the AARP will dramatically increase. Next in line is the National Rifle Association (NRA). With a membership approaching 3 million and a budget of $87 million (ranking it behind only the AARP and AMA in terms of annual expenditures), the NRA is one of the most active and effective interest groups in the nation.

The least advantageous position an interest group can be in is to have both low membership and funding levels. The NAACP has only 345 thousand

**TABLE 5.1** Political Interest Groups—Membership and Budgets

| Group | Number of Members | Budget (in Millions) |
|---|---|---|
| American Association of Retired Persons (AARP) | 33,000,000 | $305 |
| American Federation of Labor-Congress of Industrial Organizations (AFL-CIO) | 13,000,000 | 62 |
| Christian Coalition | 1,600,000 | 25 |
| National Rifle Association (NRA) | 2,650,000 | 87 |
| Sierra Club | 650,000 | 39 |
| National Association for the Advancement of Colored People (NAACP) | 345,000 | 16 |
| American Medical Association (AMA) | 300,000 | 205 |
| Common Cause | 270,000 | 11 |
| U.S. Chamber of Commerce | 180,000 companies | 70 |
| Tobacco Institute | 13 companies | 38 |

*Source:* Public Interest Profiles, 1994–1995 (Washington, DC: Congressional Quarterly, 1994).

> **The NRA Strikes Back**
>
> Outraged by legislation authorizing a waiting period on handgun purchases and mandating a ban on assault weapons, the National Rifle Association responded by contributing more than $3 million to Republican congressional candidates in 1994. Tens of thousands of NRA members worked the phones, distributed campaign literature, and knocked on doors. Their efforts appear to have paid off. Of 24 "priority" races they concentrated on, the NRA won 19. More significantly, perhaps, 224 members of the new Republican-controlled House of Representatives—a majority—are given an "A" approval rating by the NRA.

members and a budget of only $16 million, while Common Cause has 270 thousand members and a budget of only $11 million.

Another factor that determines interest group effectiveness is the *level and quality of the organizational structure*. Employees, mailing lists, fundraising activities, communications systems, and membership recruitment are relevant factors in assessing organizational quality.[8] Enthusiasm for a cause can also go a long way in overcoming a relatively modest budget. The Christian Coalition is a case in point. Relying upon "leadership schools" to train recruiters, the Coalition emphasizes a grassroots approach that seeks to establish a cadre of at least 10 workers in each of the nation's 175,000 political precincts. The group has also developed a "rapid-response network" connected by phone, fax, and modem across the country that has the capacity to generate tens of thousands of calls and letters to public officials almost immediately.

## PUBLIC PERCEPTIONS OF INTEREST GROUPS

In the abstract, Americans do not evaluate interest groups favorably. One poll found that 69 percent of the respondents felt that interest groups have too much influence over the political process. A survey conducted by CBS News/New York Times discovered that 71 percent thought that most members of Congress were more interested in serving special-interest groups than in serving the people they were elected to represent. However, "special-interest" is a loaded term. When Americans are asked about particular groups, they are much more favorable in their evaluation. A Gallop poll found that 93 percent felt positively about the American Cancer Society. A majority of the respondents also gave positive evaluations to Planned Parenthood (82 percent), National Organization of Women (71 percent), National Rifle Association (58 percent), National

---

[8] Andrew S. McFarland, *Common Cause: Lobbying in the Public Interest* (Chatham, NJ: Chatham House, 1984).

Right to Life Commission (55 percent), Handgun Control (55 percent), and the American Civil Liberties Union (54 percent). Only the Tobacco Institute received a negative evaluation (26 percent of the respondents rated it favorably).[9]

## INTEREST GROUP TACTICS

Interest groups attempt to influence public policy through lobbying, electioneering, public relations campaigns, and protest demonstrations.

### Lobbying

Lobbyists engage in a variety of activities to influence public policy. They frequently testify before congressional committees and other government agencies. In their testimony, they present highly detailed and often technical information and data on complex issues. They introduce the findings of research reports and studies conducted by their interest group. Through the provision of information, lobbyists seek to influence the deliberations and choices of public officials.[10]

Lobbyists also rely upon an extensive network of contacts with government officials. It is a truism in Washington that "they come to govern, they stay to lobby." By way of illustration, 48 of the 121 lawmakers who left Congress after the 1992 election had become lobbyists after a year. Fifty of their top assistants, and more than 30 senior members of the Bush Administration, had become lobbyists as well. These former congressmen and executive branch officials rely upon their friends and colleagues in government to gain access. Once obtained, that access is used to make a case for their interest group's position and perspective on relevant policy issues.

Lobbyists also seek to influence lawmakers through an array of informal social activities. They have lunch together, attend the same receptions and parties, and play golf on weekends. Even a poker game can have significant political implications. For years, a small group of influential lobbyists—representing banks, securities firms, credit unions, and other financial institutions—regularly played poker with Senator Alfonse D'Amato (Republican, New York), chair of the Senate Banking Committee. It was a high-stakes game (winnings reached as much as $400 a hand) in which Senator D'Amato often won. What did the lobbyists win? Two of the regular players represented the Securities Industries Association, as well as individual securities firms. Was it a coincidence that Senator D'Amato recently approved legislation making it more difficult for investors to sue brokers and companies that issue stock? Another

---

[9] Alan Rosenthal, *The Third House: Lobbyists and Lobbying in the States* (Washington, DC: Congressional Quarterly Press, 1993), p. 6.
[10] Lester W. Milbrath, *The Washington Lobbyists* (Chicago: Rand McNally, 1963).

lobbyist who participated represented the corporation that manufactures Sweet'n Low, whose main ingredient is saccharin. In 1977, the Food and Drug Administration banned saccharin as a suspected carcinogen. However, Senator D'Amato has sponsored legislation that has blocked the ban. Still another player was a lobbyist for an association of debt collectors. Senator D'Amato obtained Senate approval of legislation that weakened governmental control over debt collectors.[11]

## Efforts to Control Lobbyists

The General Accounting Office estimates that only a third of the 14 thousand lobbyists working in Washington are registered. Others believe that the actual number of lobbyists is much higher—ranging from 18 to 60 thousand. Until recently, no one knew for sure. Now, they will. In the first legislation of its kind enacted since 1946, Congress has passed a lobbyist disclosure bill. The provisions of the new law require that lobbyists report their clients, disclose the issues they lobbied on, list the agencies and branch of government they lobbied, and estimate the amount of money they were paid. Even lobbyists who advise clients on lobbying strategy—rather than engaging in direct contacts with lawmakers—will be required to register. Lobbyists who represent corporate clients before federal agencies—such as the Environmental Protection Agency—will similarly be covered by the law. Lawyers (previously exempt) will also have to register as lobbyists and disclose the required information. Failure to file semi-annual reports and provide information on lobbying activities carries a penalty of $50,000 in fines. For disclosure purposes, any person spending at least 20 percent of their time lobbying—or who is paid for more than one lobbying contact in six months—is considered a lobbyist. In response to Republican objections, however, disclosure is not required for "grassroots" lobbying that uses computerized direct mail and other high-tech methods to generate phone calls and letters to lawmakers.

Combined with an earlier decision banning gifts to members of Congress, the lobbyist disclosure bill represents the most significant lobbying legislation ever enacted by Congress.[12] Although the new law does not restrict what lobbyists can do, the required public disclosure of their activities, clients, and expenditures will likely exert an important impact upon their behavior.

## Electioneering

Another tactic employed by interest groups is electioneering. If money talks, lawmakers hear the interest groups loud and clear. Approximately half of the

---

[11] *New York Times,* "Lobbyists Had Access to D'Amato at Weekly Private Poker Games," (October 25, 1995).

[12] Helen Dewar and Michael Weisskopf, "Lobbyist Disclosure Bill," (*Washington Post,* November 30, 1995).

Lobbyists line the back wall of the Texas State Senate. (Source: Texas Senate Media Services)

members of the House of Representatives receive 50 percent or more of all their campaign contributions from Political Action Committees (PACs). These PACs collect campaign contributions from interest groups and individuals and distribute them to political candidates. PACs contributed $180 million to House and Senate candidates in the 1992 election.

Labor union PACs spent the most ($42,558,000), followed by PACs representing Finance/Insurance/Real Estate ($28,792,000), Agriculture ($15,028,000), and Health ($14,406,000). The overall distribution of the PAC money favored Democrats and incumbents over Republicans and challengers. Some PACs distributed their contributions fairly equally between Democrats and Republicans, while others heavily favored one party over the other. For example, Agriculture PACs gave 51 percent to the Democrats and 49 percent to the Republicans, while Labor and Lawyers/Lobbyist PACs favored Democratic candidates with shares of 94 percent and 80 percent, respectively. On the other hand, Construction Industry PACs gave 62 percent of their money to the Republicans. Sometimes, PAC contributions can backfire. In 1993 and 1994, the dairy industry disproportionately gave its money to the Democrats. An analysis of dairy industry contributions by the Center for Responsive Politics, a Washington research group, found that no other agricultural industry favored the Democrats as much. Nine of the top ten House recipients of dairy industry money were Democrats. So were seven of the top ten Senate recipients. Ironically, the new Republican Congress has produced in both the House Agricultural Committee and the Senate Agricultural Committee plans to slash dairy subsidies in half, or abolish price supports all together.

Many believe that interest group money corrupts the political process. Critics of the system point to the collapse—and subsequent bailout of the savings and loan industry—as an illustration.[13] During the 1980s, lobbyists for the industry worked hard to get Congress to deregulate the savings and loan sector. Limited to financing home mortgages, the thrifts could not survive competition from banks. Deregulation would allow them to move into other areas of investment, particularly commercial real estate. When Congress deregulated the industry, the rush was on to buy land and finance the construction of many thousands of apartment buildings, shopping centers, and office complexes. When the bottom began to fall out of the commercial real estate market, government regulators became suspicious of reckless speculation, fraud, and insider dealing within numerous individual savings and loans. However, critics allege that when these officials attempted to investigate suspected wrongdoing within the industry, they were pressured to drop their inquiries by various senators and congressmen—lawmakers who had received (and continued to receive) millions of dollars in campaign contributions from savings and loan PACs. Apparently, Congress knew what industry officials were up to. Because of the huge sums of money involved, however, they looked the other way. The final cost of bailing out the collapsed industry was $145 billion, the largest financial bailout in American history. The government closed or merged 747 thrifts, protected 25 million depositor accounts, and sold off more than $465 billion in assets. The U.S. Justice Department reported that more than 3,700 senior executives and owners of savings and loans served time in prison for their crimes.

Money, however is not the only way interest groups attempt to influence the outcomes of elections. Labor unions and other organizations make phone calls and send precinct workers door to door during campaigns to get out the vote for candidates they support. The Christian Coalition passes out millions of "voter guides," many of which are distributed in church pews. Increasingly, these grassroots efforts (which include computerized mass mailouts supporting one candidate or attacking another) are a preferred interest group strategy during election campaigns.

---

[13] Kirsten Downey Grimsley, "After Closing Many Doors, Resolution Trust Corporation Shuts Its Own," (*Washington Post,* December 29, 1995).

## Public Relations Campaigns

In addition to lobbying and electioneering, interests groups also rely upon public relations campaigns to influence policy. Less direct than lobbying contacts with lawmakers and cash payments funneled into congressional campaign bank accounts, public relations campaigns seek to influence public opinion regarding a particular issue.[14] By running commercials on television and radio and buying advertisements in newspapers and magazines, interest groups hope to energize citizens to communicate with their elected representatives. For example, while Congress was debating President Clinton's proposal to reform the healthcare system, a number of groups—American Medical Association, National Federation of Independent Businesses, medical insurance companies—spent millions of dollars on advertisements opposing the plan. Money is the primary reason why more groups don't mount public relations campaigns. Advertisements broadcast or printed for a national audience are enormously expensive. Only extraordinarily well-funded organizations can afford them.

## Protest Demonstrations

Lobbying, campaign contributions, and public relations campaigns are the preferred tactics of interest groups. They are conventional, routine, and widely accepted. Protest is none of the above. It is unorthodox and unpredictable in terms of the public's reaction to it. It does not enjoy the legitimacy—nor record of success—accorded more traditional forms of interest group participation. Then why is it used at all? Why do some groups undertake sit-ins, boycotts, parades, marches, and demonstrations? Generally, groups employ protest behavior as a last resort. If more conventional tactics have failed (or can't be effectively utilized because of a lack of resources), the group may be forced to engage in protest activities in an attempt to elicit public sympathy and support.[15]

### *The United Farm Workers*

The United Farm Worker's Union, illustrates the point. Lacking the money to lobby, campaign, and buy ads on television, the union (composed primarily of Mexican-American migrant workers) under Cesar Chavez's leadership had little choice but to try something different. In 1965, Chavez and his supporters marched 250 miles to the California state capitol in an effort to generate support for their struggle against the California grape growers. Chavez also periodically engaged in fasts (one lasted for five weeks) in order to dramatize the plight of the migrant workers. As his public support grew,

---

[14] Jeffrey M. Berry, *The Interest Group Society* (Glenview, IL: Scott, Foresman, 1989).
[15] Michael Lipsky, *Protest as a Political Resource* (Skokie, IL: Rand McNally, 1970).

## Interest Group Tactics

Cesar Chavez led farm workers' boycotts. (Source: Bettmann Archive)

Chavez was finally able to call for a national boycott against the grape growers. When substantial numbers of Americans stopped buying grapes, the growers caved in. They recognized the union, and eventually accepted wage and benefit agreements for union members.

### The Anti-Abortionists

The history of the anti-abortion movement demonstrates, however, that the use of nonviolent protest can sometimes turn into violent protest. Further, the use of violence by an interest group to achieve its goals may prove counterproductive. Originally, Operation Rescue—an anti-abortion group founded in 1987—employed nonviolent measures to protest abortion. Members of the group held mass protests in front of abortion clinics, frequently blocking entrances and halting traffic. Their tactics attracted numerous members from other anti-abortion groups that had been protesting through prayer vigils and other less confrontational means.

In 1993, however, a member of Operation Rescue murdered a doctor employed at an abortion clinic in Florida. Since then four other doctors and clinic workers have been murdered, several more have been wounded, and nine attempted murders have been investigated. The militant wing of the anti-abortion movement calls doctors who perform abortions "serial killers" and "mass murderers," and argues that killing an abortion doctor is biblically sanctioned. The "Army of God" manual, a user's guide to bombing, burning, and vandalizing abortion clinics, proclaims "We, the remnant of God-fearing men and women of the United States of America do officially declare war on the entire child-killing industry."[16]

The turn toward violence has shattered the ranks of Operation Rescue. Many members—repelled by the use of violence—have dropped out. The political response has also devastated the group. In 1994, the national government passed a law making it a federal offense to block access to clinics.

---

[16] Timothy Egan, "Conspiracy Is an Elusive Target in Prosecuting Foes of Abortion," (*New York Times*, June 18, 1995).

## Women as an Interest Group—A Long and Winding Road

Denied the right to full participation in the political system, women were determined nonetheless to organize and pursue a social agenda. Relying upon religious zeal and moral commitment, they had established by the end of the first quarter of the nineteenth century a wide-spread network of organizations that raised money, built charitable institutions such as orphanages, and sponsored religious revivals. In 1834, a national women's organization against prostitution was founded. Within ten years, there were more than 400 chapters of the American Female Moral Reform Society. In their newspaper *The Advocate,* they attacked "the predatory nature of the American male who was drenched in sin." Their campaigns against illegitimacy may have had an impact. Illegitimate birth rates fell significantly during the first part of the century.

A female anti-slavery society was formed in Philadelphia in 1833, and four years later a national convention of anti-slavery women was held in New York. At a convention in Seneca Falls, New York, in 1848, women demanded full citizenship—including the right to vote. Although the demand for political rights dominated the women's movement for the next 50 years, the effort was not particularly successful. By 1900, only a few states allowed women to vote. The focus now shifted to social reform. Women's organizations lobbied effectively at both the state and local levels on behalf of social and economic legislation for women and children. Victories included the first law providing public assistance for mothers with dependent children (1911), the first minimum wage law for women and children (1912), and the creation of the children's (1912) and women's bureaus (1920) in the U.S. Department of Labor. In 1916, Congress enacted a Child Labor Law banning the products of child labor from interstate commerce (declared unconstitutional two years later by the Supreme Court).[17] The settlement house movement—which originated with Hull House on Chicago's West Side in 1889 under the leadership of Jane Addams—further illustrated the effectiveness of women's organizations during this period. Quickly spreading to cities throughout the country, these settlement houses served as community centers for immigrants and the urban poor. Providing facilities such as kindergartens and citizenship schools, the settlement houses were in the forefront of the demand for better recreational services, garbage removal, and police protection. Social work broadened the base of the women's movement. Eventually, this broadened base of support translated into at least some political progress as well. Women won the right to vote in the state of Washington in 1910, in California in 1911, and in four more states during the next three years. However, it was not until 1920 that the Nineteenth Amendment provided a constitutional guarantee of this right for all women.[18]

---

[17] Sara M. Evans, *Born for Liberty: A History of Women in America* (New York: The Free Press, 1989).
[18] William H. Chafe, *The Paradox of Change* (New York: Oxford University Press, 1991).

---
**The Rise—and Leveling Off—of an Interest Group Entrepreneur**

Ralph Nader has had an extraordinary career as a consumer advocate. He became a household word after publishing *Unsafe at Any Speed* in 1965, a book exposing the dangerous structural designs in American automobiles—particularly the Corvair manufactured by General Motors. The publicity and debate generated by the book led to the passage of the National Traffic and Motor Vehicle Act that set new safety standards for cars. Nader was off and running as an interest group entrepreneur. In 1968, he founded the Center for Study of Responsive Law which became his primary vehicle for creating other consumer advocacy organizations. Using the $425,000 he received from General Motors to settle an invasion of privacy lawsuit (the auto company had hired private investigators to discredit him after he published *Unsafe at Any Speed*) Nader organized the Center for Auto Safety. In 1970, Nader created the Congress Project to examine the operations of government, and the following year he established Public Citizen, an umbrella organization that included Congress Watch (a congressional lobbying group), and Health Research Group (a medical industry monitoring organization).*

In the following years, Nader and his "raiders" played a major role in the creation of the Consumer Product Safety Commission (1972), in strengthening the Freedom of Information Act (1974), in getting the Supreme Court to rule that minimum fees for legal services violate antitrust laws (1975), in pressuring the Food and Drug Administration to ban red dye number 2 as a possible carcinogen (1976), and in getting a law passed requiring airbags in new cars.

Then, however, Nader's momentum clearly slowed. The growing conservative mood in the country—as reflected in the election of Ronald Reagan as president—ensured that consumer affairs issues would be accorded lower priority. In the early 1970s, a Gallop poll found Nader among the ten most admired Americans. A decade later, fewer than 40 percent of respondents regarded him highly. Although Nader made a brief run for the presidency as a write-in candidate in 1992, his high-water mark had passed. Substantial damage was done to his reputation in 1989 when he waged a national campaign on talk shows to prevent pay raises for members of congress. The incident cost him considerable support in Congress, including some of his closest allies.†

---
* Jeffrey M. Berry, *Lobbying for the People* (Princeton, NJ: Princeton University Press, 1977).

† Anthony Ramirez, "Nader Remains Unbent by Winds of Change," (*New York Time:* December 31, 1995).

## The Environment and Interest Groups

When the Republicans took control of Congress after the 1994 elections, they vowed to relax federal laws governing air and water pollution, toxic wastes, safe drinking water, wildlife protection, and management of federal lands for industrial uses such as mining and timber production. The Republicans in the House of Representatives have already enacted revisions to the Clean Water

## An Evangelical Interest Group Entrepreneur

William Lloyd Garrison took his mission in life seriously. Denouncing the Constitution's recognition of slavery as "a covenant with death, an agreement with Hell," he was moved to publicly burn a copy in 1854, declaring, "So perish all compromises with tyranny." Devoting his entire career to a fight against slavery, he was jailed in 1830 for libeling a New England businessman involved in the domestic slave trade. He began publishing the *Liberator*—an antislavery weekly—in 1831, and the following year he formed the New England Antislavery Society. Not even ministers and the Holy Scripture were immune from his increasingly bitter attacks upon those individuals and institutions that did not share his hatred of slavery. Like many "true believers," Garrison was both egotistical and self-righteous. In the first issue of the *Liberator* he wrote,

> I will be harsh as truth and as uncompromising as justice. I am in earnest—I will not equivocate—I will not excuse—I will not retreat a single inch—AND I WILL BE HEARD.

When Garrison joined forces with other groups to form the American Antislavery Society, the abolitionist movement developed a powerful momentum. The group employed two primary strategies to achieve its goals.

First, the abolitionists conducted a massive public relations campaign that included large public rallies, smaller gatherings sponsored by local chapters, and home visits by agents of the movement. The abolitionists also seized upon the latest developments in communications technology. The first American interest group to utilize mass mailings, the Antislavery Society distributed 100 thousand pieces of literature in 1834 and more than a million the following year. Undertaking a "great postal campaign," the abolitionists literally flooded the nation—including the South—with antislavery pamphlets, mailing out 175 thousand in a single month from the New York City post office alone.

The second strategy was directed against the government. Local chapters were encouraged to bombard Congress with petitions demanding that action be taken against the institution of slavery. In 1836, 30 thousand of these petitions were sent, and by 1838 Congress had been inundated with more than 500 thousand signed petitions.

One of the fastest growing interest groups in American history, the number of local antislavery societies increased from 200 in 1835 to more than 500 in 1836. By 1840, there were 2 thousand chapters with 200 thousand members. Growing from an original base of Quakers, free blacks, writers, and evangelical Christians, the group quickly expanded into a broad-based, middle-class movement.

The American Antislavery Society would not be the last interest group to effectively combine evangelical fervor, mass mailings to both individuals and public officials, and a grassroots approach to chapter building and membership drives. These tactics are identical to the ones employed today by Ralph Reed's Christian Coalition.

> **The Lawyers Lose**
>
> Money does not always work. Despite contributing $40 million in 1994 to state and national candidates (mostly Democrats), lawyers face the likelihood that Congress will reform personal injury and product liability law. Concerned about the size of settlements in these types of cases (a woman was awarded $2.7 million when she was burned by a hot cup of McDonald's coffee), the Republican-controlled Congress may well impose restrictions on the suits that can be brought as well as set limits on the size of settlements. The trial lawyers aren't panicking yet. Observes one of their number, "Politics are very, very strange. One election, the other fellow beats your candidate, and two years later, the new fellow's knocking on your door looking for some money."
>
> Various interest groups have pushed tort reform—as the issue is known—to the center of the legislative agenda. Consumer advocate groups see personal injury and product liability laws as essential in their struggle against dangerous and irresponsible business practices and products. According to this perspective, large damage awards have made numerous products safer, including children's sleepwear that is treated with flame retardants, cars that now have rear-seat safety belts, chainsaws that are now equipped with safety guards, and farm tractors that have antiroll-over bars. Consumer advocate groups argue that the cost of safer products is low. Damage awards in a typical year total only $4 billion, or about a penny for every dollar of profit earned by the nation's corporations.
>
> Supporters of tort reform believe that this figure is ridiculously low. When legal fees, unrecorded out-of-court settlements, litigation costs, the time lost by executives and employees, and the absence of worthy products that do not come on the market are taken into account, the real costs are at least $100 billion, and may reach as high as $300 billion—or 30 cents to 85 cents for every dollar of profit. The size of damage awards also appears to be rising. According to the Rand Corporation, the median damage award in Cook County, Illinois (Chicago), increased from $1.9 million during the period 1984–1989 to $6.8 million during 1990–1994.

Act that voided many of the law's cleanup requirements for industry. Further, both the House and Senate are considering legislation that would scale back requirements for cleaning up toxic waste sites under the superfund program. However, none of the major changes in environmental protection and regulation proposed by the Republicans have become law. Many—perhaps all—of these proposed changes will eventually be defeated. Why?

The political power of environmental interest groups is a major factor.[19] Their impact is so significant that President Clinton recently assured the leaders of more than two dozen of the largest environmental organizations that he would veto any bills that substantially weakened environmental protection.

---

[19] Allan J. Cigler and Burdett A. Lomis, (Eds.) *Interest Group Politics,* 3d ed. (Washington, DC: Congressional Quarterly Press, 1991).

Observes one Republican policy analyst, "Environmental groups are not the old unsophisticated bunch of dope-smoking hippies. It's big money, big politics, big consultants, big polling." Republican officials expected that their initiatives in the area would be opposed by environmental groups. What they did not anticipate, however, was that their proposed changes in environmental laws would also be opposed by traditionally supportive interest groups. When Republicans introduced legislation that would give states the opportunity to take control of 270 million acres of federal land, it ran into powerful opposition from some unexpected directions: the National Rifle Association and groups representing hunters and sportsmen. Fearing that they would be denied hunting access if federal ownership was abolished, these interest groups undertook a public relations campaign to coincide with the opening of deer and elk season. "Keep Public Lands in Public Hands," announced their barrage of radio ads. The bill's Republican sponsors now admit that even they wouldn't vote in favor of the proposed legislation.[20]

## New Groups on the Block

Asian-Americans have been particularly active in establishing their own interest groups in recent years. Several factors have accounted for this development. First, the growing numbers of Asian-Americans, in conjunction with their high level of educational and professional attainment, have raised their political consciousness. Second, congressional consideration of legislation to reduce the level of legal immigration has mobilized the Asian-American community like no other issue. Finally, organizational efforts have been encouraged by the rise in hate crimes. A study conducted by the National Asian Pacific-American Legal Consortium, an organization that represents 40 groups, found that there was a 35 percent increase in anti-Asian hate crimes nationwide, up from 335 incidents in 1993 to 452 incidents in 1994.

These groups employ traditional tactics to achieve their goals. Asian-Americans have recently staged peaceful demonstrations in New York, San Francisco, and Los Angeles, undertaken voter registration drives, lobbied lawmakers, initiated letter-writing campaigns, taken out full-page advertisements in the Washington Post urging defeat of the immigration bill, and raised money for those political candidates who support their agenda.

The Asian American Association—only a year old and already claiming a membership approaching 400 thousand—is typical of the new breed of interest group. Besides aggressively pursuing a political agenda, the association has modeled itself after the American Association of Retired Persons. It offers its members discounts on car rentals, auto club memberships, insurance, English

---

[20] Tom Kensworthy and Gary Lee, "Divided GOP Falters on Environmental Agenda," (*Washington Post,* November 24, 1995).

lessons, toys, and books. It even offers computer software in Mandarin, Japanese, Korean, Vietnamese, and Tagalog.[21]

## Conclusion

Alexis De Tocqueville got it right when he wrote about the importance of associations in American life. According to the famous Frenchman, groups served a vital function in a democratic society. They made weak men strong.

> In aristocratic societies men do not need to combine in order to act, because they are strongly held together. Every wealthy and powerful citizen constitutes the head of a permanent and compulsory association composed of all those who are dependent upon him or whom he makes subservient to the execution of his designs. Among democratic nations, on the contrary, all the citizens are independent and feeble; they can do hardly anything by themselves, and none of them can oblige his fellow men to lend him their assistance. They all, therefore, become powerless if they do not learn voluntarily to help one another . . . As soon as several of the inhabitants of the United States have taken up an opinion or a feeling which they wish to promote in the world, they look out for mutual assistance, and as soon as they have found one another out, they combine. From that moment they are no longer isolated men, but a power seen from afar, whose actions serve for an example and whose language is listened to.[22]

## POLITICAL PARTIES

### The Functions of Political Parties

The current two-party system has lasted so long (almost a century-and-a-half) because it works. It is exclusive enough to offer viable policy choices and alternatives, and sufficiently inclusive to provide a means of representation for groups and individuals. Political parties perform the following functions in society:

1. Nominate candidates.
2. Spend money to elect candidates.
3. Stimulate interest in elections by taking policy positions, creating controversy, and encouraging potential voters to participate.
4. Serve as a cue to voting; simplify voting choices. Most voters know that the Democrats are more liberal and the Republicans more conservative.

---

[21] Steven A. Holmes, "Anti-Immigrant Mood Moves Asians to Organize," (*New York Times,* December 12, 1995).
[22] Alexis de Tocqueville, *Democracy in America* (New York: Mentor Books, 1956), p. 156.

5. Develop a following among the electorate; serve as a source of political and ideological association and identification for voters.[23]
6. Inform and educate voters; call attention to and identify issues and problems.
7. Offer policy proposals and alternatives; help set the public agenda.
8. Run the government.
9. Serve as a focus of opposition when not in power.
10. Serve as an organizational focus for and source of unity for interest groups.
11. Provide voters with a means for holding public officials accountable.

## The Decline of Political Parties

Although political parties continue to play an important role in the American political system, they are not as significant as they once were.[24] Several factors are responsible for this development. Political parties once built and maintained loyal followings through the provision of jobs and a variety of social welfare services. With the institutionalization of civil service and the rise of the welfare state, however, the ability of the parties to manipulate patronage and services in exchange for votes has been greatly diminished.

Vast public bureaucracies now deliver a variety of social welfare services—social security, medicare, welfare, foodstamps, unemployment payments—while civil service commissions administer "merit systems" to control employment decisions and patterns. Other developments have also greatly weakened political parties at the local level. The "urban reform" movement—an outgrowth of the Progressive movement during the first part of the twentieth century—initiated a series of structural changes that severely weakened political parties in many cities. These reforms included replacing a popularly elected mayor with an appointed city manager, the adoption of nonpartisan elections (candidates could no longer be identified on the ballot according to party affiliation), the elimination of patronage in city employment, and the use of at-large rather than ward or district representation.

The widespread adoption of the direct primary across the nation has also contributed to the decline of the party system. When individual voters—rather than party leaders—have the power to directly select the party's nominees in primary elections, the candidates' reliance on the party organization is reduced. The rise of split-ticket voting has also had an impact. When voters have the choice of picking and choosing among candidates of different parties, the winner-take-all factor is eliminated.

---

[23] Kay Lawson, (Ed.), *Political Parties and Linkage* (New Haven: Yale University Press, 1980).
[24] Martin P. Wattenberg, *The Decline of American Political Parties* (Cambridge, MA: Harvard University Press, 1990).

Television has also been identified as playing a role in the decline of political parties. Allegedly, television's emphasis upon candidate image—and the lack of attention given to issue position and party affiliation—have reduced the significance of the party system. Similarly, the new technology of campaigning is also thought to have an effect. The use of polls, computers, mailing lists, specialized fund raising, political consultants, and media experts have apparently lessened the importance of party for voters as well as candidates. Voters are no longer as dependent upon the parties for information, while candidates are likely to turn elsewhere for money and other forms of support.[25]

## Party Identification

Much has been made of the fact that in recent years an increasing number of voters identify with neither major political party. Instead, they classify themselves as "independents." Is it really the case, however, that partisan identification with the Republicans and Democrats is undergoing a period of decline? The answer depends upon how one interprets poll results. For example, when respondents are simply asked to express their party preference, the results reveal that those identifying themselves as "Independent" have substantially increased in recent decades. Three-fourths of respondents identified with one of the major political parties from 1952 to 1964. Since 1970, however, two-thirds or less have. The proportion of Independents has grown from one-fifth or more of the electorate in the 1950s to one-third or more in the 1970s and 1980s.

These results, however, can be misleading. Respondents are given the choice of identifying themselves as "pure" Independents, or as Independents who "lean" toward one of the major parties. Many analysts argue that the "leaners" should, in fact, be counted as party partisans. This conclusion is based on the finding that Independent leaners vote very much like those individuals who identify with the Republicans or Democrats. When "leaners" are added to the Republican and Democratic totals, the results reveal that partisan identification with one of the major political parties remains remarkably high. No more than 15 percent of Americans have ever identified themselves as actual Independents (in the mid-1970s). Currently, almost 90 percent of respondents classify themselves as Republican or Democratic partisans, while only 10 percent identify as Independents.[26]

## Republican Growth

One thing is clear. The Republicans are getting stronger in terms of voter identification. In 1964, 60 percent of respondents expressed a partisan identification

---

[25] William Crotty, *American Parties in Decline* (Boston: Little, Brown, 1984).
[26] Steven E. Finkel and Howard A. Scarrow, "Party Identification and Party Enrollment," *Journal of Politics, 47* (May, 1985): 620–42.

with the Democrats, while only 30 percent classified themselves as Republicans. Recently, however, the Democratic share of the electorate has declined to 50 percent, while the percentage of Americans identifying with the Republicans has increased to 40 percent. With the Reagan landslide in 1984 and Bush's victory in the Gulf War, the percentage of respondents expressing a partisan preference for the Republicans exceeded 40 percent.

An important factor in this shift from Democrats to Republicans is the South. In 1952, approximately 70 percent of white southerners identified themselves as Democrats, while less than 20 percent classified their party affiliation as Republicans. Four decades later, only 37 percent identified as Democrats, while 25 percent saw themselves as Republicans and 38 percent classified themselves as Independents. In addition, the western states are much more Republican than previously.

## Group Identification

Women favor the Democratic Party by a margin of 5 to 10 percent. More than 80 percent of blacks also favor the Democrats. In fact, no group gives a larger margin of preference to one party over the other. Hispanics also strongly identify (by more than three to one) with Democrats over the Republicans. Republican identifiers tend to be upper income and better educated while Democratic partisans are lower income and less well educated. Republican supporters include professionals, managers, white-collar workers, retired persons, and women who don't work outside the home. Democratic supporters are blue collar, labor union members, and women who do work outside the home. Religion also plays a role. Protestants tend to be Republicans, while Catholics and Jews are more likely to identify with the Democrats. Republicans, however, sometimes win a quarter of the Jewish vote and 40 percent of the Catholic vote.

Carol Moseley Braun, a Senate candidate, speaks at the National Organization for Women convention. (Source: AP Photo)

## Ideological Unity

Republicans reveal less diversity in their political beliefs than Democrats. For example, 55 percent of Republicans identify themselves as conservatives, 17 percent as moderate, and only 8 percent as liberal. By contrast, 24 percent of Democrats see themselves as liberal, 22 percent identify as moderates, and 19 percent identify as conservatives. It

**TABLE 5.2** Third-Party Candidates

| Candidate | Year | % of Vote | Electoral Votes |
|---|---|---|---|
| Eugene Debs | 1912 | 6.0 | 0 |
| Theodore Roosevelt | 1912 | 27.4 | 88 |
| Robert La Follette | 1924 | 16.6 | 13 |
| George Wallace | 1968 | 13.5 | 46 |
| John Anderson | 1980 | 6.6 | 0 |
| Ross Perot | 1992 | 18.9 | 0 |

would be wrong to assume, however, that all Republicans are of a like mind. Even Republican primary voters—considered the most conservative part of the electorate—are divided on a number of issues. A New York Times/CBS poll conducted in 1995 found, for example, that on the abortion issue 38 percent of the expected Republican primary voters were "pro-choice" while 33 percent were "pro-life." Three out of four believed that the Republican Party should not support a constitutional amendment prohibiting abortion, eight out of ten do not belong to the "religious right," and only one out of five said they would be more likely to support a candidate if leaders of the religious right endorsed that candidate. Further, 55 percent of the respondents believed that it was necessary to have laws preventing discrimination in hiring and promotion.

## Third Parties

Third parties do not fare well in the American political system.[27] Only one third-party candidate in this century—Theodore Roosevelt running as the nominee of the Bull Moose Party—has won as much as 20 percent of the vote (see Table 5.2). It should also be pointed out that Roosevelt had already been elected President as a Republican. The best showing by a third-party candidate since Roosevelt was Ross Perot in 1992. Despite the media attention given to his campaign, however, and the vast amounts of money and grassroots effort expended on Perot's candidacy, he received only 19 percent of the vote. Most significantly, perhaps, he failed to carry a single state. Therefore, Perot received no electoral votes. Why do third-party candidates find it so difficult to compete with the major political parties? The answer includes the following factors:

- Unlike many European countries, the United States does not have a system of proportional representation. Under a proportional scheme, legislative seats are allocated in proportion to the percentage of total votes received. Consequently, all but the most minor parties are generally guaranteed at least some level of representation. In the American system, however, the

---

[27] Steven J. Rosenstone, Roy L. Behr, and Edward H. Lazarus, *Third Parties in America* (Princeton, NJ: Princeton University Press, 1984).

candidate receiving a plurality of the votes cast wins the election. The candidates who come in second or third get nothing—no matter how close they come to winning.

- The public funding of campaigns also benefits the two major parties and puts other candidates at a distinct disadvantage. Third-party presidential candidates have to wait until after the general election is over to receive their federal funds. Even then they must have received more than 5 percent of the vote. After meeting this requirement, third-party candidates are compensated in proportion to their total vote. Major party candidates, on the other hand, are paid very substantial amounts of money as soon as they are nominated.

- State laws require that third-party candidates must obtain a long list of signatures in order to get their names placed on the ballot. The two major parties in a state are automatically placed on the ballot if their party won a minimum number of votes in the last election.

- A basic consensus in American society further operates to the detriment of third-party candidates. According to this perspective, the absence of a feudal tradition has contributed to a lack of class conflict. Further, the nation's political system emphasizes moderation, pragmatism, and compromise. Instead of ideological confrontation, most Americans are thought to share a basic consensus with respect to important values. Since most voters are positioned at the center of the political spectrum, the two major parties also locate themselves near the middle of the distribution in order to attract electoral support.[28] As a result, third parties are at a disadvantage. If they attempt to compete with the major parties for the broad middle, they will be overwhelmed. If they position themselves near the extreme ends of the political distribution (either left or right), there will be too few votes to make a difference.

Third parties find it difficult to survive because the two major parties often steal their ideas and co-opt their positions on issues. For example, the Democrats incorporated into their own platform many of the programs and policy proposals initially championed by the Populist, Progressive, and Socialist parties. Similarly, Republicans eventually claimed as their own several of the issues and ideas first articulated in 1968 by George Wallace and the American Independent Party.

## Party Organization

The two major parties are generally organized along similar lines. The National Committee is composed of party officials from each state and territories. The

---

[28] Benjamin I. Page, *Choices and Echoes in Presidential Elections* (Chicago: University of Chicago Press, 1978).

The Republican National Convention in 1996 was held in San Diego. (Source: Gamma Liason)

Republican National Committee has 160 plus members, consisting of the national committeeman, national committeewoman, and the party chairperson from each state, the District of Columbia, Guam, Puerto Rico, and the Virgin Islands. The Democratic National Committee has more than 400 members, consisting of the two national committee members and the party chairs from each state. The Democratic National Committee assigns the number of committee members from each state on the basis of the state's population and the state's past support for Democratic candidates. The chairs of both the Republican and Democratic National Committees are picked by the party's presidential nominee and elected by the committees.[29]

The National Conventions, held every four years, are attended by thousands of delegates. They nominate candidates for president and vice president, adopt party platforms, and decide upon rules and regulations to run the party organization. Since 1968, the Democrats have emphasized fairness and equity in representation in their delegate selection process. At the 1968 Democratic

---

[29] Paul S. Herrnson, "Re-Emerging National Party Organizations," in L. Sandy Maisel, (Ed.) *American Parties* (Boulder, CO: Westview, 1990).

National Convention in Chicago, antiwar protesters forced the party to reform the procedures by which delegates were picked. Following that national convention, the party leadership took steps to significantly increase the number of female and minority delegates. Democratic state delegations are now equally divided between male and female representatives. In 1982, the party also decided that a share of convention delegates should be reserved for party leaders and elected officials. These so-called "superdelegates" now comprise about 15 percent of all delegates at the national convention. The intent of this reform was to include party leaders and officials whose advice and support were considered essential to electoral victory.

Before each new session of Congress, the Democrats and Republicans in each House hold Congressional Party Conferences to elect party leaders and decide upon committee assignments. These party conferences (called a "caucus" by House Democrats) are devoted entirely to party issues and matters within the House of Representatives and Senate. These Congressional Party Conferences are not related to or associated with the national committees.

The Republican and Democratic senators and representatives in Congress also operate Congressional Campaign Committees to raise money for congressional candidates. Independent of the national committees, there are separate Republican and Democratic campaign committees in both the House and Senate.

## A Decentralized Party System

The American party system is highly decentralized. The national committees exert no control over party activities in the House and Senate. Democrats and Republicans in the Congress set their agendas and pursue their policy goals with no guidance or direction from the national party organization. Similarly, the national leadership exerts little control over state and local party and campaign activities. The Republican National Committee and Democratic National Committee don't even control their respective presidential campaigns. Candidates build and direct their own organizations to compete in party primaries and win delegates. Even the party's presidential nominee controls his own campaign.

The party system in the United States is highly decentralized, consisting of a very loose coalition of independent parts. The national party organizations, the congressional party conferences, the congressional campaign committees, the state parties, the local parties, and the individual candidates running for office all essentially pursue independent paths. They gather together once every four years to nominate presidential and vice-presidential candidates, write a party platform, and develop rules and regulations for the national organization. Then they disperse again, likely to maintain only a minimal level of contact and coordination during the course of the next four years.[30]

Despite this level of decentralization, these loose-knit party alliances seem to work remarkably well. At the national level and in all 50 states, the two-party system defines issues, structures debate, calls public attention to problems and issues, helps develop the political agenda, gets out the vote, stimulates interest and awareness, nominates candidates, runs campaigns, raises money, develops coalitions of interest groups, provides an ideological and political focus for countless millions of American citizens, proposes policy solutions and alternatives,[31] enhances public responsiveness and accountability, serves as a source of opposition when not in power, and runs thousands of governments at all levels of American life—cities, counties, states, and national.

## CONCLUSION

The American party system provides an organizational and ideological focus for opposing alliances of likeminded interest groups. These political groups pool their numbers and resources and work within the party system to elect candidates, achieve policy goals, and gain control of government at the local, state, and national levels. Political parties play a crucial role in the American political system. They not only nominate candidates, define issues, conduct election campaigns, and run the government, they also provide a means for the electorate to hold public officials accountable.

## RECOMMENDED READINGS

### Interest Groups

Berry, Jeffrey M. 1989. *The Interest Group Society.* Glenview, IL: Scott, Foresman.

Berry, Jeffrey M. 1977. *Lobbying for the People.* Princeton, NJ: Princeton University Press.

Cigler, Allan J., and Burdett A. Loomis, Eds. 1991. *Interest Group Politics in America.* Washington, DC: Congressional Quarterly Press.

Lowi, Theodore J. 1979. *The End of Liberalism.* New York: Norton.

McFarland, Andrew S. 1984. *Common Cause: Lobbying in the Public Interest.* Chatham, NJ: Chatham House.

Olson, Mancur. 1965. *The Logic of Collective Action.* Cambridge, MA: Harvard University Press.

Rosenthal, Alan. 1993. *The Third House.* Washington, DC: Congressional Quarterly Press.

Sabato, Larry J. 1984. *PAC Power: Inside the World of Political Action Committees.* New York: Norton.

---

[30] Cornelius Cotter and Bernard C. Hennessey, *Politics Without Power* (New York: Atherton, 1964).

[31] Gerald M. Pomper, *Elections in America* (New York: Longman, 1980).

Schlozman, Kay Lehrman, and John T. Tierney. 1986. *Organized Interests and American Democracy.* New York: Harper & Row.

Schattschneider, E. E. 1960. *The Semi-Sovereign People.* New York: Holt, Rinehart and Winston.

Truman, David B. 1951. *The Governmental Process: Political Interests and Public Opinion.* New York: Knopf.

Walker, Jack L. "The Origins and Maintenance of Interest Groups in America," *American Political Science Review* (June, 1983): 390–406.

## Political Parties

Black, Earl and Merle Black. 1987. *Politics and Society in the South.* Cambridge, MA: Harvard University Press.

Epstein, Leon. 1986. *Political Parties in the American Mold.* Madison: University of Wisconsin Press.

Herrnson, Paul S. 1988. *Party Campaigning in the 1980's.* Cambridge, MA: Harvard University Press.

Jewell, Malcolm E., and David M. Olson. 1988. *Political Parties and Elections in American States.* Chicago: Dorsey Press.

Kayden, Xandra and Eddie Mahe. 1985. *The Party Goes On: The Persistence of the Two-Party System in the United States.* New York: Basic Books.

Key, V. O. 1964. *Politics, Parties, and Pressure Groups.* New York: Thomas Y. Crowell.

Maisel, Sandy, Ed. 1990. *The Parties Respond.* Boulder, CO: Westview Press.

Polsby, Nelson W. 1983. *Consequences of Party Reform.* New York: Oxford University Press.

Pomper, Gerald M. Ed. 1984. *Party Organization in American Politics.* New York: Praeger.

Price, David E. 1984. *Bringing Back the Parties.* Washington, DC: Congressional Quarterly Press.

Rosenstone, Steven J., Roy L. Behr, and Edward H. Lazarus. 1984. *Third Parties in America: Citizen Response to Major Party Failure.* Princeton, NJ: Princeton University Press.

Sabato, Larry J. 1988. *The Party's Just Begun: Shaping Political Parties for America's Future.* Glenview, IL: Scott, Foresman.

Sarauf, Frank J., and Paul Allen Beck. 1988. *Party Politics in America Glenview,* IL: Scott, Foresman.

Shafer, Byron E. 1988. *Bifurcated Politics: Evolution and Reform in the National Party Convention.* Cambridge, MA: Harvard University Press.

Sundquist, James L. 1983. *Dynamics of the Party System.* Washington, DC: The Brookings Institution.

Wattenberg, Martin P. 1988. *The Decline of American Political Parties, 1952–1988.* Cambridge, MA: Harvard University Press.

# 6

# *Political Minorities*

| | |
|---|---|
| Native Americans<br>   *The West*<br>Blacks<br>   *A Brief History*<br>   *The Reaction*<br>   *Poverty and Welfare*<br>   *Income*<br>   *Jobs*<br>   *White Myths/Black Truths* | Hispanics<br>   *Mexican-Americans*<br>   *Puerto Ricans*<br>   *Cubans*<br>Women<br>Gays<br>Conclusion |

I did not know then how much was ended. When I look back now from this high hill of my old age, I can still see the butchered women and children laying heaped and scattered all along the crooked gulch as plain as when I saw them with eyes still young. And I can see that something else died there in the bloody mud, and was buried in the blizzard. A people's dream died there. It was a beautiful dream . . . the nation's hoop is broken and scattered. There is no center any longer, and the sacred tree is dead.
—Black Elk, on the Massacre at Wounded Knee

Sails furled, flag drooping at her rounded stern, she rode the tide in from the sea. She was a strange ship, indeed, by all accounts, a frightening ship, a ship of mystery. Through her bulwarks black-mouthed cannon yawned. The flag she flew was Dutch; her crew a motley. Her port of call, an English settlement, Jamestown, in the colony of Virginia. She came, she traded, and shortly afterwards was gone. Probably no ship in modern history has carried a more portentous freight. Her cargo? Twenty slaves.
—J. Saunders Redding

There is no greater nor more enduring contradiction in all our shared experience as a people than the one between the sacred national pledge of equality under the law on the one hand, and the treatment of racial and political minorities on the other. The nation could pass an amendment promising equal protection of the laws and ignore it, vow that all are created equal and reject it, sign a solemn treaty and break it. The torturous path followed by the Republic's minorities in their quest for a measure of the political and economic success offered by the American Dream is paved with glorious rhetoric and strewn with broken promises.

The minority experience is not one that flows from the wellspring of what Abraham Lincoln called "the better angels of our nature." And yet the record also reflects a remarkable degree of progress. It is perhaps the most enduring promise of the unfinished Republic that each generation will try anew to live up to standards—that were it not for those better angels—would be impossibly high.

## NATIVE AMERICANS

When Europeans arrived on the North American continent, five to seven million Indians already lived there, grouped into several hundred tribes and speaking two thousand different dialects. There were the Micmac, the Abnaki, the Pennacook, the Massachusetts and Narraganset, the Tuscarora and Catawba and Yamasee and Calusa. Further west lived the Algonquin, the Mohawk, the Iroquois, Ottawa, Illinois, Miami, and Sioux. For three hundred years, the white settlers would war against these Native Americans for control of the continent. One English clergyman wrote in 1585 that three goals should motivate the settlement of Virginia: To plant the Christian religion, to traffic in goods, and to conquer.

The Indians quickly recognized their intentions. The chief of the Powhatans announced to the settlers at Jamestown in Virginia, "You have come here not to trade but to invade my people and possess my country." His successor attacked Jamestown in 1622 and killed 347 of the inhabitants. The colonists responded with a vengeance. The war lasted until 1634 and inaugurated a new era in Anglo-Indian relations. As white settlements pushed throughout southern New England, the Indians fought back. The Pequots, in particular, refused to yield. A single Puritan attack on one of their villages led to the massacre of 500 Pequot men, women and children. A militiaman who participated observed that "God laughed at the Enemies of his People, filling the Place with Dead Bodies." Eventually, the entire tribe was exterminated. The few survivors were sold into slavery in the West Indies.

Other tribes continued the war against the encroaching English. King Philip of the Wampanoag lead a coalition of tribes against the English in a war that began in 1675. Five percent of the entire adult white population in Massachusetts and Rhode Island were killed during the next two years, and 20 percent of the settlements in these two states where either destroyed or their inhabitants forced to flee. The Indians suffered more severe losses. Five thousand of them—30 percent of the native population in the region—died from wounds, disease, and starvation.

The bitter warfare against the native population for control of the land presented a major paradox for the Puritans. How could they reconcile their Christian beliefs with the systematic use of violence against the Indians. They would ask themselves, "By what right or warrant can we enter into the land of the Savages and take away their rightful inheritance from them and plant ourselves in their places?" But just as their religion prompted them to question what they were doing to the Indians, that same religion provided them with ample justification. "Be fruitful, and multiply," said the Bible, "and replenish the earth, and subdue it." They saw themselves as God's "chosen People." And just as God had driven the tribes out of Canaan for the benefit of the Israelites, so he was now driving the Indians before the Puritans. An epidemic that decimated the Indian population in 1633 prompted John Winthrop to write, "If God were not pleased with our inheriting these parts, why did he drive the natives before us? And why doth he still make room for us by diminishing them as we increase?"[1]

These religious doctrines would continue to provide a rationale and justification for policies toward the Indians well into the nineteenth century. In 1874, Samuel Harris, Professor of Theology at Yale University, observed that God traditionally selected a "Chosen People" as an agent through which to work His will. According to Professor Harris, it was the Anglo-Saxon race "more than any other that the world is now indebted for the propagation of Christian ideas and Christian civilization." Thirteen years later, James King, a prominent Protestant minister, noted that God had chosen the Anglo-Saxons "to conquer the world for Christ by dispossessing feeble races and assimilating and molding others." Another influential clergyman of the period, Josiah Strong, wrote that "this race is destined to dispossess many weaker ones, assimilate others, and mould the remainder, until in a very true and important sense, it has Anglo-Saxonized mankind."[2]

The colonial wars against the Indians degenerated into barbarism on both sides. In 1694, the Massachusetts General Court enacted a law that provided a bounty to be paid for the killing or capture of a hostile Indian. It was total war and by the end of the seventeenth century, the eastern seaboard had been largely cleared of Indian resistance. A thriving business was done in the selling of Indian slaves, with thousands sold into slavery in both the colonies and West Indies. In the Carolina colony in 1708, the population numbered 5,300 whites, 2,900 African slaves, and 1,400 Indian slaves.

Although the tribes in the interior escaped extermination, their culture was profoundly changed as well. European diseases devastated their populations. Alcohol was heavily used. Increasingly, they grew dependent upon manufactured products such as guns. Further, the dynamics of the fur trade

---

[1] Forrest G. Wood, *The Arrogance of Faith* (New York: Harper & Row, 1990).
[2] Wood, *The Arrogance of Faith*.

fundamentally altered the relationships among the interior tribes. As the competition for animal pelts to barter for guns and alcohol grew more intense, the tribes became more aggressive against their neighbors. The Iroquois eventually conquered the Erie, Huron, Susquehannah, and Delaware. Within individual tribes, the attributes of the warrior came to be valued over the skills of the farmer and the artisan. Since women had traditionally played a major role in tribal agriculture, females suffered a loss of status in many Native American communities.

The Indian wars raged throughout the eighteenth century, against the Catawba, Chickasaw, Choctaw, Creek, and Cherokee in the South; against the Delaware in Pennsylvania; and against the Iroquois in New York. Given the Indians' past experience with the colonists, it is not surprising that most of the tribes fought on the side of the British during the Revolutionary War. It was a major mistake. Having allied themselves with the losers during the struggle for independence, the Iroquois were forced, once the war ended, to cede all their lands west of New York and Pennsylvania to the United States. The Chippewa, Ottawa, and Wyandot were required to cede lands that would eventually become the state of Ohio.

The various tribes would subsequently renounce these treaties, and in 1790 and 1791 an alliance under the leadership of the Shawnee administered major defeats to American military forces. Retribution was swift in coming. When the western tribes were defeated by General "Mad Anthony" Wayne at the Battle of Fallen Timbers, settlers flooded the interior. A decade after the battle, Ohio boasted a population in excess of 100,000. Many thousands more poured into Indiana and Illinois. Deceit, bribes, and threats were widely used to steal additional millions of acres of Indian land that had not already been ceded by treaty.

Chief Tecumseh of the Shawnee forged another coalition of western and southern tribes to resist the white encroachment upon their lands. This alliance was religious as well as military in nature. In part, it was a reaction to and a rejection of the Christian doctrines that had been spread among the Indians by the missionaries. The alliance also reflected a revival of traditional tribal religions. The warriors came to believe that the white man's weapons could not harm them. They soon learned otherwise. In 1811, William Henry Harrison, Governor of the Indiana Territory, defeated the Indian Confederacy at Tippecanoe.

The election of Andrew Jackson as president in 1828 would prove to have horrendous consequences for several Indian tribes. His military reputation rested to a considerable extent on his success in fighting and killing Indians, and he did little to conceal his hatred for them. To Jackson the Indians were not only barbaric, they represented a major obstacle to the advance of American civilization. His past behavior toward them did not bode well for the types of policies he would pursue as president. In 1814, he defeated the Creeks and took more than twenty million acres of their land for the government. He would later write that "I have long viewed treaties with the Indians an absurdity not to be reconciled to the principles of our government."[3]

As president, Jackson set about dealing with the problem presented by the five so-called "civilized tribes"—the Chickasaw and Choctaw in Mississippi, Alabama, and Tennessee; the Cherokee and Creek in Georgia and Alabama; and the Seminole in Florida. Their traditional tribal grounds included vast tracts of rich soil greatly coveted by the cotton planters. Unfortunately, efforts to dispossess the tribes of their land was complicated by the fact that they were protected by various federal treaties. Jackson's Administration quickly found a way around this inconvenience. Jackson simply withdrew the federal troops responsible for enforcing the treaties, thereby subjecting the tribes to state law. The state of Georgia declared that the Cherokee did not constitute a nation, that the tribe consisted of nothing more than individuals who were mere tenants on land owned by the state. This decision was quickly copied by other states. President Jackson also supported the Indian Removal Act of 1830 which forced the Indians to accept treaties providing for the exchange of their eastern lands for territory west of the Mississippi River. Combined with the use of military force, the Removal Act accounted for the eviction of all but the Cherokee and the Seminole by 1837. The Seminole fought a long and bitter war against the United States, while the Cherokee were given until 1838 to depart. In that year, General Winfield Scott herded 15 thousand Cherokee into concentration camps. Marched to the Oklahoma Territory during the winter months in an ordeal that became known as the Trail of Tears, 4 thousand died on the route. The extermination and forced relocation of the southeastern tribes was complete.

## The West

> Of all the promises the white man made to us, he kept just one. He promised to take our land, and he took it.
>
> Indian Chief

After the Civil War, the settlement of the American West began in earnest. Mighty forces were at work. The press of population from the already settled midwestern states, immigrants from Europe hungry for land, gold seekers, and land speculators exerted enormous pressure on the western territories. In addition, the construction of the transcontinental railroad dramatically enhanced access to this vast area. The national government also provided a powerful incentive. The Homestead Act of 1862 offered families 160 acres of free land. These policies were enormously successful. Between 1870 and 1900, more new

---

[3] Quoted in Robert V. Remini, *The Life of Andrew Jackson* (New York: Harper & Row, 1988).

land was cultivated than in the past 250 years. Over a million residents of the midwestern states moved West. Kansas boasted a population of 850 thousand citizens in 1880, and in 1882 alone more than a 100 thousand Scandinavian immigrants settled in the region. The population of the Dakota Territory rose from 20 thousand in 1873, to 135 thousand in 1880, and 550 thousand in 1885. Between 1878 and 1887, almost 25 million acres of Dakota land were settled by homesteaders. By 1900, half of the nation's cattle and sheep, three-fifths of its wheat production, and a third of its cereal crops were grown on farms and ranches located in the new western territory. More than 15 thousand miners had rushed to the Black Hills in the Dakota Territory by 1880. During the next century, the Homestake Mining Company would produce more gold than any other mine in the hemisphere.

The insatiable demand for land and gold sealed the doom of the western tribes. The Frenchman Alexis de Tocqueville had been correct when he had written that "the European is to the other races of men what man in general is to the rest of animate nature. When he cannot bend them to his use or make them indirectly serve his well-being, he destroys them and makes them vanish little by little before him."[4]

Ironically, the various tribes had long enjoyed legal protection. During the presidency of Andrew Jackson, the Supreme Court had handed down a series of decisions in which it held that Indian tribes are "domestic dependent nations." These nations retained all sovereign powers, were largely autonomous and free from the jurisdiction of state governments, and subject only to the ultimate authority of the national government. Unfortunately for the Indians, President Jackson and subsequent administrations simply ignored the Supreme Court's rulings.

The hundreds of separate treaties provided little protection. By 1860, the resettled eastern tribes were forced to give up their lands in Kansas and Nebraska and relocate even further west. In 1867, the government developed a program to essentially clear the western territory of the Indian obstacle. The new approach emphasized the "civilizing" of the Indian. He would be educated, Christianized, and transformed into a peaceful farmer. To this end, two major reservation areas were designated. Part of the Dakota Territory was set aside for the Northern Plains tribes—then Sioux and Cheyenne—while the Oklahoma Territory was designated for the Southern Plains Indians, plus the Choctaw, Cherokee, Chickasaw, Creek, and Seminole. This new treaty arrangement was broken as quickly as the previous ones. The discovery of gold in the Black Hills of Dakota in 1874, the refusal of the military to stop the influx of miners onto these Indian lands, and the subsequent defeat of General Custer (who had been sent to eliminate Indian resistance to the influx of white

---

[4] Alexis de Tocqueville, *Democracy in America* (New York: Mentor Books, 1956).

settlers), provided the government with the pretext to finally break the power of the Northern Plains tribes and take more of their land.

In 1887, another major step was taken in the effort to separate the tribes from their traditional nomadic ways and send them down the "white man's road." In that year, Congress passed the General Allotment Act—the Dawes Act—which provided that each Indian family head would receive 160 acres of land. The land would be held in trust by the government for 25 years after which time the owner was free to use or dispose of the land as he saw fit. A clause in the legislation also provided that the "surplus" Indian lands left after each family received its 160 acres would be purchased by the government at extremely low prices. Some recognized that the Dawes Act was nothing more than another monumental land grab.

The Indians were headed toward disaster even if there had been no Dawes Act, even if the government had lived up to its treaty obligations, even if the military had not sent tens of thousands of soldiers against them. They were doomed because the buffalo was doomed. Between 1872 and 1874 more than 4 million buffalo were slaughtered by white hunters in the Kansas Territory alone. In only a few years, herds that had numbered as many as 60 million animals had been annihilated. Killed for their hides and tongues, the carcasses were left to rot. Some settlers helped pay the note on their homestead mortgage by collecting the bones which were sold for fertilizer and glue.[5]

Once the buffalo were gone, the Plains tribes had little choice but to submit to efforts to civilize them. Congress passed legislation extending the jurisdiction of the federal courts to include major crimes committed on the reservations. The government also outlawed religious dances and ceremonies, placed restrictions on various marriage practices and relationships, and established Indian police and courts. Major emphasis was placed upon education. In an effort to "kill the Indian, save the man," off-reservation boarding schools—such as the Carlisle Indian Industrial School—were created. Although the intent was to equip the Indian with the skills to compete in the white world, the actual outcome was a great deal different. One graduate of the boarding school system concluded that "Most girls found their life's work in city kitchens and most boys who did not drift back to the reservation lost their identity in a shop." Although the schools established on the reservation were better attended, this was due in part to the fact that the government handed out rations to Indian children between six and fourteen years of age only if they were attending school. With the buffalo gone, the tribes were dependent on government rations and handouts. With tribal traditions shattered, they were forced into dependency on their conqueror's educational system. With native religions outlawed, they turned to the white man's God. As one Sioux chief put it,

---

[5] Marc Reisner, *Game Wars* (New York: Viking, 1991).

"When the white man came he had the Bible and we had the land. Now we have the Bible and he has the land." Few Native Americans felt that it had been a good trade, much less a fair one. Perhaps Mark Twain put it best when he wrote, "The time has come when blood-curdling cruelty has become unnecessary. Inflict soap and a spelling book on every Indian that ravages the plains and let them die."

One desirable piece of land that had so far escaped the fate that had befallen most tribal lands was two million acres located in the Indian Territory of Oklahoma. Highly fertile and greatly coveted by white settlers, government resistance to robbing the Indians of still more of their land finally collapsed in the face of continuous public demand. In 1889, the "Boomers" flooded the territory and claimed the land as their own. It was all gone in a matter of hours. Loss of other tribal lands continued throughout the West. The Indians owned 138 million acres in 1887. By 1934, their holdings had been reduced to 55 million. Most of this was desert.

The Supreme Court finally confirmed in law what the government had long practiced in fact. In 1903, in the *Lonewolf* case, the Kiowa, Comanche, and Apache tribes brought suit to prevent the Secretary of the Interior from disposing of lands that the tribes had previously ceded to the government for $2 million dollars. The Indians argued that the prior agreement was not legally binding since the government had failed to obtain the signatures of three-quarters of the adult males as required by an 1868 treaty. Although the government admitted that the required signatures had not been gathered, the Supreme Court refused to rule in favor of the tribes. Instead, the Court held that Congress possessed absolute power over the Indians, that this power included the right to "abrogate" any treaties that had been entered into, and that this power "had always been deemed a political one, not subject to be controlled by the judicial department of the government." In the *Lonewolf* case, the Court ruled that while tribal lands were secure from encroachment by individual states and citizens, no such protection from the federal government existed. In essence, Congress had the authority to turn Indian lands into cash, regardless of the owners' preferences. Finally the supreme law of the land had recognized what the Indians had always known: The government could do with the Indians and their land as it saw fit. Treaties meant nothing.

Although the Plains tribes were now broken, the remnants confined to reservations, they would try one last time to regain the old ways. A religious revival swept through the tribes, celebrated in the Ghost Dance, where the dancers went into a trance and saw the future, a future world without the white man and inhabited by many buffalo, a world cleansed and fresh again. On the Sioux reservations, the warriors came to believe that white bullets could no longer hurt them. They grew increasingly militant. The Army was dispatched to protect adjacent white settlements. When tribal police attempted to arrest one of the movement's leaders—the Medicine Man Sitting Bull—a fight broke out. Several Indians, including Sitting Bull, were killed. The Army then set out to catch one of the rebellious bands, a group of 340 Indians under the leadership of Chief Big Foot. Surrounding the band near Wounded Knee Creek on the night of December 28, 1890, was General Custer's old outfit, the Seventh Cavalry. Big Foot, dying of pneumonia, raised a white flag. The soldiers were in the process of disarming the Indians the next day when shots rang out. A soldier was killed. In the massacre that followed, almost three hundred defenseless Sioux were slaughtered. Two hundred of them were women and children.

Government policy toward Native Americans changed after World War I. In part, this was the result of gratitude for the patriotic service of thousands of Indians who served in the military during the war. The policy changes that occurred could also be attributed to the growing recognition that the programs of assimilation and land allotment had been abject failures. Finally, there developed an increased awareness on the part of policymakers of the intrinsic worth of tribal values and cultural norms. The Indian Citizenship Act which bestowed citizenship status on all Indians born in the United States was enacted in 1924. Further, the policy of assimilation was abandoned in favor of an approach that came to be known as "cultural pluralism." While not forsaking the hope that the Indian would eventually discover a comfortable niche in white society, public officials now accepted that uniquely tribal practices and traditions were entitled to nurturing and protection.

With the election of Franklin Roosevelt in 1932 and the appointment of John Collier as his Commissioner of Indian Affairs, the concept of cultural pluralism was implemented in the form of the Indian Reorganization Act (IRA). Collier now had a grant of authority from the president to develop a "New Deal" for the Indians. Specifically, this new deal stopped the practice of allotment that had operated to drastically reduce tribal land holdings. The IRA also greatly enhanced tribal autonomy. Individual tribes now had the authority to adopt a constitution and bylaws, elect a tribal council, hire legal counsel, borrow money from a credit fund, control the disposition of tribal lands, and engage in negotiations and agreements with state and local governments.

But the emphasis upon cultural pluralism and tribal self-determination during the 1920s and 1930s gave way in the postwar years to still another shift in federal policy toward the Indians. During the 1950s, the national paranoia generated by McCarthyism and the widespread fear of Communism created conditions conducive to an emphasis upon homogeneity and conformity. There was little support for addressing the special needs of Native Americans. In fact, many whites came to regard the communal, noncapitalist nature of tribal society as a threat to conventional, mainstream values such as individualism, competition, and capitalism. The pendulum had now swung back in the direction of assimilation. Opposition developed to the notion that the government should encourage tribal autonomy, foster self-determination, and adopt programs to nurture and protect the uniqueness and separateness of Indian life. President Harry Truman's Commissioner of Indian Affairs threw his support behind these policy shifts. Having previously headed the War Relocation Authority which administered the internment of Japanese-Americans during World War II, Dillion Meyer and the "terminationists" sought to abolish the Indian Bureau and transfer its functions—such as health and education—to state and local governments. Their efforts were successful. In 1953, Congress passed a resolution stating "termination" to be government policy. The intent was to terminate the status of Native Americans as "wards" of the government.[6]

In that same year, Congress also enacted legislation providing that jurisdiction over criminal offenses and certain civil cases would now be controlled by individual states rather than by the tribes themselves or the federal government. Although the law applied only to California, Minnesota, Nebraska, Oregon, and Wisconsin, provision was also made for other states to assume similar jurisdiction over Indian Affairs simply by passing legislation to that effect. Since state governments tended to be less supportive of Indian objectives—and decidedly less sensitive to tribal needs and problems—this new legislation struck a significant blow at tribal autonomy and self-determination.

Criticizing the reservations as concentration camps, Commissioner Meyer also implemented a program to relocate Native Americans to the city. As a result of an extensive public relations campaign, 35 thousand Indians migrated to the cities during the decade of the 1950s. Fewer than 3,500 became permanent members of the workforce. Many more joined the ranks of the unemployed and impoverished.

In the 1960s, Indians living on reservations had a life expectancy of less than 44 years, 20 years less than the national average. In many tribes, 80 percent of all families received an income below the poverty level. Only 20 percent of the adults had a high school education, and only a third were employed. The infant mortality rate for Indians was 30 percent above the national average. The suicide rate was extraordinarily high.

The reservations did benefit from the War on Poverty programs and expenditures of the 1960s. Head Start, for example, enjoyed some success. However, the decade was more notable for the increasing political activism of Native Americans, particularly among those living in the cities. According to Edward Lazarus,

> Amid poverty and petty criminality, coping with alcoholism . . . city Indians found their shared ethnic identity—regardless of tribal affiliation—to be a rare source of strength and community. Around the Indian centers that cropped up

---

[6] Edward Lazarus, *Black Hills/White Justice* (New York: HarperCollins, 1991).

in every city with a native population, in the jails and bars and pool halls they steeped themselves in their common histories of grievance and celebrated a resurgent sense of cultural identity. Having witnessed the black civil rights movement . . . hearing now the angry and powerful rhetoric of a Stokely Carmichael or Malcolm X, watching the rising tide of the movement against the Vietnam War, many city Indians embraced the politics of militancy and united under the banner of Red Power. Almost overnight, American Indians became Native Americans, who vowed in strident terms to reclaim their rights and heritages.[7]

Organized into groups, such as the American Indian Movement (AIM), the political activities of Native Americans grew increasingly militant. In 1969, a group of 78 Indian students took control of Alcatraz, a deserted island in San Francisco Bay that had been used as a federal prison until 1963. They issued the following proclamation:

> We feel that this so-called Alcatraz Island is more than suitable for an Indian Reservation, as determined by the White Man's own standards. By this we mean that this place resembles most Indian reservations in that:
>
> 1. It is isolated from modern facilities, and without adequate means of transportation.
> 2. It has no fresh running water.
> 3. It has inadequate sanitation facilities.
> 4. There are no oil or mineral rights.
> 5. There is no industry, and so unemployment is very great.
> 6. There are no health care facilities.
> 7. The soil is rocky and unproductive, and the land does not support game.
> 8. There are no educational facilities.
> 9. The population has always exceeded the land base.
> 10. The population has always been held as prisoners and kept dependent on others.
>
> Further, it would be fitting and symbolic that ships from all over the world, entering the Golden Gate, would first see Indian land, and thus be reminded of the true history of this nation. This tiny island would be a symbol of the great lands once ruled by the free and noble Indians.

Although the occupants of Alcatraz were removed by federal marshals in 1971, their protest dramatized the plight of Native Americans, and inaugurated an era of Indian nationalism. Widespread media coverage of the incident invoked the moral support of sympathetic whites. For the first time, many Americans became aware of the conquest of Indian lands, the annihilation of numerous tribes, and the destruction of native cultures. Books such as Vine

---

[7] Lazarus, *Black Hills/White Justice*.

A band of Sioux Indians laid claim to Alcatraz Island in 1969. (Source: UPI/Bettmann)

Deloria's *Custer Died for Your Sins* and Dee Brown's *Bury My Heart at Wounded Knee*[8] brilliantly portrayed the tragic consequences of white settlement, chronicled the noble if doomed resistance of the tribes, and celebrated native values and traditions.

Legally, at least, Native Americans made substantial progress during the period. The Voting Rights Act and Fair Housing Act eliminated racial barriers to full political participation and home ownership. In 1968, Congress enacted the Indian Civil Rights Act which effectively repealed the "termination" legislation of the previous decade. The Civil Rights Act required tribal consent

---

[8] Dee Brown, *Bury My Heart at Wounded Knee* (New York: Henry Holt, 1970).

before state governments could assume jurisdiction over Indian affairs. The Act also extended most of the restrictions and prohibitions contained in the Constitution's Bill of Rights to tribal governments. One notable exemption was the First Amendment's requirement of separation of church and state. The pendulum had essentially swung. The emphasis in the new legislation was upon a growing recognition that "cultural pluralism is a source of national strength."

In addition to the Civil Rights Act, Congress also enacted the Indian Self-Determination and Educational Assistance Act which strengthened tribal control over the education of the young. By 1980, the national government was appropriating $2 billion a year for Indian programs and services. In the 1970s, the Supreme Court handed down rulings upholding tribal authority in civil matters such as the regulation of alcohol on the reservation. In general, various judicial decisions upheld the right of tribal authorities to govern Indians living on the reservation. The Court also voided the attempts of state governments to levy taxes on Indian property and income. By almost any measure, therefore, Native Americans had experienced significant legal gains. However, economic and social conditions on the reservation had not kept pace. In recent years, many of the poorest counties in the nation have been Indian. Many Native Americans live in houses without electricity, running water, and indoor plumbing. On many reservations, up to 80 percent of the adults are unemployed. On others, it is not uncommon for fully one-half of all adults to be alcoholics. On one reservation, alcoholism among pregnant women had resulted in permanent prenatal brain damage in one out of every four babies. Incidents of domestic violence, drug abuse, child neglect, and suicide are extraordinarily high. The proportion of adult Indian deaths under the age of 45 is considerably above the national average.

Native Americans, more than any other group, bore the consequences of the playing out of those powerful forces that shaped the American Republic: Conquest, manifest destiny, racial and moral superiority, the sanctity of private property, military invincibility, and a sense of a divinely inspired mission. That these things could have been done by a people who took deep pride in their Christian heritage makes the eventual outcome all the more ironic and astounding. Nowhere was the enormous contradiction between Christian ideals and the powerful impulse of national self-interest more starkly portrayed than at the Battle of Wounded Knee. Dee Brown in his book *Bury My Heart at Wounded Knee* writes,

> The wagonloads of wounded Sioux (four men and forty-seven women and children) reached Pine Ridge after dark. Because all available barracks were filled with soldiers, they were left lying in the open wagons in the bitter cold while an inept Army officer searched for shelter. Finally the Episcopal mission was opened, the benches taken out, and hay scattered over the rough flooring. It was

the fourth day after Christmas in the Year of our Lord 1890. When the first torn and bleeding bodies were carried into the candlelit church, those who were conscious could see Christmas greenery hanging from the open rafters. Across the chancel front above the pulpit was strung a crudely lettered banner: PEACE ON EARTH, GOOD WILL TO MEN.

## BLACKS

> What happens to a dream deferred?
> Does it dry up
> Like a raisin in the sun?
>
> Langston Hughes

> It was a strange religion, this christianity, which taught equality and brotherhood and at the same time introduced on a large scale the practice of tearing people from their homes and transporting them to a distant land to become slaves.
>
> John Hope Franklin,
> *From Slavery to Freedom*

Fully a quarter-of-a-century ago, the National Advisory Commission on Civil Disorders concluded that "our nation is moving toward two societies, one black, one white, separate and unequal." For all but a small part of the black population, their prophesy has come to pass. Increasingly, the term "permanent black underclass" has entered the national discourse about race and poverty. The problems of poverty, unemployment, drugs, violence, welfare, and racism appear so intractable that many have abandoned hope that the society has either the will or the means to do anything about them. Fifty years ago, Gunnar Myrdal wrote that "Segregation is so complete that the white Southerner never sees a Negro except as his servant and in other standardized and formalized caste situations."[9]

### A Brief History

The Civil War freed blacks from one kind of slavery and delivered them into another. This new form of bondage was economic as well as political. Reduced to the status of serfs by the system of tenant farming, southern blacks were completely dependent upon the land, supply, and credit practices of landlords and local merchants. Violence and other forms of political intimidation were employed to augment the coercive effects of an agricultural system that grossly inhibited the accumulation of economic assets, education, and skills. The

---

[9] Gunnar Myrdal, *An American Dilemma* (New York: Harper and Brothers, 1944).

coalition of blacks and poor whites forged by the Populists caused the white power structure to react with a vengeance. Segregation of public facilities—hospitals, prisons, colleges, hotels, railroad passenger service, recreational areas—was legal throughout the southern states. Literacy tests, poll taxes, and educational and residency requirements were enacted to prevent blacks from voting. Even as late as 1880, after Federal occupation troops had been withdrawn, 70 percent of black males voted in many southern states. Between 1896–1904, however, the 130 thousand black voters in Louisiana had fallen to only 1,300. Black voter registration in 1954 was only 5 percent in Mississippi, 11 percent in Alabama, and 19 percent in Virginia.[10] This repressive political system condoned the systematic use of violence as well. Between 1900–1930, more than 1,600 blacks were lynched. Roger Ransom and Richard Sutch write that,

> In 1865 emancipation from chattel slavery permitted black Americans one kind of freedom. No one would deny that this freedom was a significant and meaningful one. With their freedom blacks advanced their material income and their economic welfare. They gained a degree of independence that was significantly greater than they were allowed in bondage. Yet this freedom was incomplete. Unlike the indentured servants of Colonial America, blacks received no freedom dues: land redistribution was aborted and the blacks were forced to begin their lives as free men and women without money, without tools, without work animals, without assets of any kind. Their economic, political, and social freedom was under constant attack by the dominant white society determined to preserve racial inequalities. The economic institutions established in the post-emancipation era effectively operated to keep the black population a landless agricultural labor force, operating tenant farms with a backward and unprogressive technology . . . Slavery produced a largely illiterate black population and left it an easy victim of racial oppression. Perhaps the vulnerability of an illiterate black population was recognized, for black education became a primary target of white oppression. The costs of education and skill acquisition were increased by acts of violence and discrimination.[11]

World War I was a major catalyst for change. More than 400 thousand black soldiers served in the military, and thousands fought against the Germans in France. The mobilization effort also created unprecedented economic opportunities. In addition, restrictions on immigration provided jobs for southern blacks in industrial cities that ordinarily would have gone to white ethnic groups. Four hundred thousand blacks left the South for northeastern and midwestern cities during the war years in one of the greatest human migrations in

---

[10] James A. Morone, *The Democratic Wish* (New York: Basic Books, 1990).
[11] Roger Ransom and Richard Sutch, *One Kind of Freedom* (Cambridge: Cambridge University Press, 1977), p. 198.

the nation's history. Henry Ford sent recruiting agents to the South to find blacks to work in his auto plants. He transported them north on trains commissioned for that purpose and paid them at the extraordinary rate of $5 per day.

Between 1880–1900, only 38 thousand blacks left the five cotton states of Louisiana, Alabama, Mississippi, South Carolina, and Georgia for nonsouthern destinations. Between 1910-1930, however, more than 670 thousand departed. The black population of Chicago alone grew from 44 thousand in 1910 to 109 thousand in 1920, and 234 thousand in 1930. Although this out-migration was massive, it accounted for only 15 percent of the 4.6 million blacks living in the five cotton states. Many continued to eke out a living as sharecroppers, almost totally dependent on landlords and local merchants for supplies and credit. Martin Luther King, Jr. visited a southern plantation in 1965 and encountered black sharecroppers who were still paid in scrip rather than money. They had never seen U.S. currency. The movement north increased during the Depression and gained momentum thereafter. Almost a half million blacks migrated from the south during the 1930s, 1.58 million in the 1940s, and another 1.6 million in the 1950s.[12]

Since emancipation, black Americans have pursued a number of different strategies in an effort to obtain a fuller measure of political and economic freedom. Booker T. Washington emphasized accommodation and hard work. He believed that blacks should strive to excel within the existing system. Merit would be rewarded once whites recognized their determination to succeed. W. E. B. DuBois believed that a more aggressive strategy was required. He doubted that the simple virtues of hard work and perseverance would be sufficient to compel fundamental political and economic change. DuBois advocated an approach that would nurture and develop a black intellectual and leadership elite. Education and the attainment of political skills were essential goals. Under his leadership, the National Association for the Advancement of Colored People (NAACP) was established in 1911.

Marcus Garvey encouraged a more confrontational approach. Convinced that racism provided the best explanation of the black community's degraded economic, social, and political condition, Garvey found the solution to that condition in black power and an emphasis upon a sense of racial identity and solidarity. Rejecting the notion that blacks could ever reach an accommodation with whites, he advocated separatism instead. His emphasis upon black nationalism would presage a similar strategy of black power pursued in the 1960s.

One of the most successful political strategies was the one pursued in the federal courts. Court decisions struck down the white primary in 1944, outlawed housing covenants that prohibited selling to blacks (1948), ruled against

---

[12] Nicholas Lemann, *The Promised Land* (New York: Knopf, 1991).

Civil rights supporters in Washington, DC during the 1963 freedom march. (Source: National Archives)

laws establishing segregation on interstate bus lines (1946), and held segregated public schools to be unconstitutional (1954). The nonviolent protest movement led by Martin Luther King, Jr., culminated in the Civil Rights Act of 1964 and the Voting Rights Act of 1965. The Civil Rights Act guaranteed equal access to public accommodations, prohibited discrimination in employment, created the Equal Employment Opportunity Commission, and gave the Attorney General broad power to enforce the provisions of the law. The Voting Rights Act struck down literacy tests, and provided for the registering of voters by federal officials in counties where less than half of the minority residents were on the voting rolls. As we can see in Table 6.1, these legislative victories dramatically increased the number of black officeholders.

Despite these major legal victories, many blacks grew increasingly disenchanted with what they considered to be largely symbolic gains. Little had been done, they argued, to change the actual distribution of income, wealth, employment opportunity, and power in society. Whites, on the other hand, became less supportive of black demands. When Martin Luther King, Jr. marched in Chicago's neighborhoods in 1965, his efforts were much less successful than

**TABLE 6.1** Number of Black Elected Officials by Type of Office

| Year | Total | U.S. and State Legislature | City and County | Law Enforcement | Education |
|---|---|---|---|---|---|
| 1970 | 1,479 | 179 | 719 | 213 | 368 |
| 1973 | 2,635 | 256 | 1,268 | 334 | 777 |
| 1976 | 4,006 | 299 | 2,284 | 415 | 1,008 |
| 1979 | 4,636 | 315 | 2,675 | 491 | 1,155 |
| 1982 | 5,241 | 342 | 3,017 | 573 | 1,309 |
| 1985 | 6,312 | 407 | 3,689 | 685 | 1,531 |
| 1988 | 6,793 | 424 | 4,089 | 738 | 1,542 |
| 1991 | 7,455 | 473 | 4,496 | 847 | 1,629 |
| 1993 | 7,984 | 561 | 4,819 | 922 | 1,682 |

*Source:* U.S. Bureau of the Census, *Statistical Abstract of the United States, 1994* (Washington DC: U.S. Government Printing Office, 1994).

they had been when he protested legal segregation in the South. The profound divergence of black and white attitudes remains. In a poll conducted in 1991, respondents were asked if there were already enough laws to help blacks, or if more legislation was needed. Significantly, 64 percent of blacks felt more legislation was needed. However, only 35 percent of whites held the same opinion. Another question in the poll asked if fairness in education, hiring, and promotion could be achieved without quotas. Only 26 percent of blacks believed that quotas were unnecessary. Fifty-nine percent of whites felt that way.[13]

The national government's "War on Poverty" also had a major, if unintended, impact upon the civil rights movement. Authorized by legislation enacted in 1964, the poverty program included the Job Corps, a loan program for rural businessmen and farmers, and Head Start. The goal of the Job Corps was to provide ghetto youths with the training and skills that would allow them to compete for employment in the private sector. Head Start was established to provide educationally deprived children with basic learning skills. The poverty war was administered by the Office of Economic Opportunity. In turn, Community Action Agencies (CAAs) were created to coordinate the various poverty programs at the local level. The legislation also provided that the program beneficiaries were to participate to the "maximum feasible extent." As originally written, this provision of the war on poverty had relatively little significance. As it developed, however, the "maximum feasible" requirement would prove to have important consequences. Black leaders in cities around the country seized upon this provision and demanded representation on the CAAs. Initially, the mayors refused to relinquish control over a program that they saw as another major source of patronage. Eventually, however, blacks

---

[13] Andrew Hacker, *Two Nations* (New York: Scribners, 1992).

gained control of the CAAs in a score of cities, and dominated the CAA staffs in many others.[14]

The poverty program came to serve as a focal point of civil rights activity in northern cities. The CAAs functioned as a power base for a new generation of community-based black leaders. This new institutional and organizational structure provided a mechanism whereby black neighborhood groups could mount and sustain a challenge to entrenched political and bureaucratic elites at city hall. They also encouraged participation in the black community, and spun off a number of other organizational and agency efforts and initiatives including neighborhood health centers, community outreach programs, parents' groups, and area councils.

One success of the poverty program was Neighborhood Legal Services. Millions of citizens were given legal counsel, and a number of significant class-action suits were brought and won. For example, the legal services program played a major role in convincing the courts to abolish residency requirements as a condition of welfare eligibility. However, the most important long-term consequence of the poverty war had little to do with poverty. In fact, little progress was made in this regard. Specific programs such as Head Start did prove to be an enduring success. However, it was the impact upon the political organization and mobilization of the black community that would distinguish the poverty program's contribution to the civil rights movement. It provided the first major source of patronage for black leaders. Control over the distribution of jobs and money gave black leaders the ability to forge political coalitions and alliances, to reward supporters, to stimulate participation, and to mobilize the minority community. In short, it provided local black leaders with the organizational resources essential to creating and sustaining a power base. The CAAs functioned as the black equivalent of the urban political machines that had responded to the needs of white ethnic groups of an earlier era. Many of the elected black officials today gained their first political experience working in the poverty program.

### The Reaction

The optimism generated by the civil rights movement of the 1950s and early 1960s was shortlived. The willingness of many whites to support black demands for a dismantling of the southern system of legal segregation did not extend to further demands for a basic restructuring of the nation's political and economic institutions. Sympathetic whites had little to fear from legislation that prohibited discrimination in voting and public accommodations. They increasingly perceived that they had much to fear from proposals that countenanced the redistribution of opportunity and income. Conservatives were

[14] Lemann, *The Promised Land*.

quick to exploit a growing concern that the government had done enough for blacks. According to Thomas and Mary Edsall in their book *Chain Reaction,* conservatives such as George Wallace "portrayed the civil rights issue not as the struggle of blacks to achieve equality—a goal increasingly difficult to challenge on the moral basis—but as the imposition on working men and women of intrusive 'social policies' by an insulated, liberal, elitist cabal of lawyers, judges, editorial writers, academics, government bureaucrats, and planners."[15]

The Edsalls argued that a number of developments operated to drive the white electorate to the right. These included the shift of the civil rights protest to the North (King's marches in Chicago), the growth of the militant "black power" movement, and the outbreak and spread of the ghetto riots. Other factors included the dramatic growth in the welfare rolls, the confrontation between white officials and black leaders over control of the War on Poverty Programs, and the extraordinary increase in crime rates. From 1960 to 1966, the crime rate grew by more than 60 percent, and between 1966 and 1971 it increased by another 83 percent. The arrest rate of blacks on homicide charges rose by more than 130 percent from 1960 to 1970. Blacks account for only 12 percent of the population, but 61 percent of the arrests for robbery, 55 percent of the arrests for murder and manslaughter, and 43 percent of the arrests for rape. Forty-five percent of the inmates of federal and state prisons are black.

Julius Wilson in his book *The Truly Disadvantaged* offers a compelling explanation for the predicament of blacks in the inner city. First, he argues, job loss in the central city has severely crippled black economic progress. In turn, the extraordinarily high rates of male unemployment make it impossible for many black men to support a family. As a result, the high incidence of female-headed families traps many blacks in the poverty/welfare cycle. The second explanation involves the escape of the black middle class from the ghetto. With the departure of successful black families, the poor blacks left in the inner city lost a powerful role model. Socially and economically isolated, this black underclass is reduced to coping with a "tangled pathology" of crime, drugs, unemployment, and female-headed households.[16]

Another book, however, received more public attention. In *Losing Ground,* Charles Murray blamed the condition of the black underclass on federal welfare programs. According to Murray, the black family fell apart and unemployment dramatically increased because the ease with which a welfare check could be obtained made work and family unnecessary. Crime rates rose because the likelihood of punishment declined. Educational achievement deteriorated because misguided public officials no longer insisted upon rigorous standards.[17]

---

[15] Thomas Edsall and Mary D. Edsall, *Chain Reaction* (New York: W.W. Norton, 1991).
[16] Julius Wilson, *The Truly Disadvantaged* (Chicago: University of Chicago Press, 1987).
[17] Charles Murray, *Losing Ground* (New York: Basic Books, 1984).

TABLE 6.2  Poverty Percentage by Race

| Year | White (%) | Black (%) |
|---|---|---|
| All persons | 8.8 | 31.9 |
| All children | 15.9 | 44.8 |
| All families | 8.1 | 29.3 |
| Female-headed households | 37.9 | 56.1 |

*Source:* Andrew Hacker, *Two Nations* (New York: Scribners, 1992).

## Poverty and Welfare

In 1991, 36 million Americans—almost 15 percent of the population—lived in poverty. In 1968, 30 percent of the nation's poor lived in center cities. In 1996, 42 percent do. Although there are as many poor whites as poor blacks, black poverty is concentrated in the inner city. Compared to only 33 percent of poor whites, 60 percent of impoverished blacks live there. The statistics are startling and frightening. An examination of Table 6.2 reveals that 45 percent of **all** black children live in poverty, but only 16 percent of white children are poor. Similarly, 30 percent of all black families are impoverished, but only 8 percent of white families are in the same economic straits. One clue is to be found in the statistics for female-headed families. A large percentage of both black and white families headed by a female (38 percent for whites and 56 percent for blacks) are poor. It is the absence of a second income earner in the home that accounts for a disproportionate share of poverty families (defined as less than $10,530 for a family of three).

The proportion of female-headed black families increased from 17 percent in 1950 to 56 percent in 1990 (Table 6.3). Significantly, the incidence of white families headed by a female has grown at the same rate, from only 5 percent in 1950 to 17 percent 40 years later. Both black and white families are experiencing major change in terms of traditional marital arrangements and patterns. The white family in 1990 is similar to the black family in 1950 in this regard. Significantly, both white and black female-headed families are prime candidates for poverty status.

TABLE 6.3  Households Headed by Women

| Year | Black (%) | White (%) |
|---|---|---|
| 1950 | 17.2 | 5.3 |
| 1960 | 24.4 | 7.3 |
| 1970 | 34.5 | 9.6 |
| 1980 | 45.9 | 13.2 |
| 1990 | 56.2 | 17.3 |

*Source:* Andrew Hacker, *Two Nations* (New York: Scribners, 1992).

Given the dramatic increase in families headed by females—and the much greater incidence of poverty among these families—it is not surprising that there has been a corresponding increase in welfare payments as well. The number of families receiving aid from Aid to Families with Dependent Children (AFDC) grew from only 644 thousand households in 1950, to 787 thousand in 1960, 1.039 million in 1965, 2.208 million in 1970, and to 3.498 million families in 1975. Welfare payments account for 65 percent of the income of female-headed households in the bottom fifth of the income distribution.[18]

One of the great myths is that welfare families live well without working. Nothing could be further from the truth. In fact, even the most generous state (Massachusetts) provided cash payments for families on welfare that averaged only $7,692 per year. This figure fell considerably short of the poverty line of $10,500. In Alabama, the comparable figure for AFDC families was a mere $1,356, with a national average of $4,644. It is difficult to imagine that a family could even survive on that amount (less than $400 per month), much less live well. Further, there is a great deal of variation across the states with respect to the percentage of single mothers (the high poverty group) receiving AFDC payments. The figure ranges from 79 percent in Wisconsin and 73 percent in Ohio, to only 34 percent in Texas and 22 percent in New Hampshire.

Almost three out of every four AFDC families have two or fewer children, and only one out of 10 such families have four or more. In addition, almost half the AFDC families have received aid for two years or less, and only 25 percent have been paid benefits under the program for more than five years. In fact, half of all beneficiaries no longer receive cash payments after two or three years in the program. The evidence suggests that this nonparticipation is voluntary. Blacks do account for a disproportionate share (40 percent) of families receiving AFDC payments. However, most of these families have only one or two children, most have received benefits for less than five years, and a majority (56 percent) are headed by females.

### Income

For a short period, there was at least some reason to be optimistic about the improving economic position of blacks. From 1963 to 1978, the gap between black and white wages fell from 45 percent to about 30 percent, a decline of one percentage point a year. But by the end of the 1970s, black wages stagnated, with the differential between blacks and whites remaining at 30 percent.[19] During the past 50 years, blacks have made up considerable economic ground. In 1939, a typical black male worker earned only $450 for every $1,000 earned by a white male worker. In 1989, that black worker was paid

---

[18] Lemann, *The Promised Land.*
[19] Edsall and Edsall, *Chain Reaction.*

$716 for every $1,000 paid a white worker. Although progress was made, the differential in earnings remains substantial. What is even more discouraging is that the progress has slowed.

The median family income in 1990 was $36,915 for whites, but only $21,423 for black families. This income gap holds for black men, even when educational levels are taken into account. For example, the black male high school dropout earns only $797 for every $1,000 earned by a white dropout. The corresponding differentials are $764 for high school graduates and $798 for college graduates. Significantly, black women fare far better than black males. They approach parity with white women for high school graduates ($942), and actually achieve parity for college graduates ($1,002).

The distribution of income within white and black families reinforces the conclusion that blacks fare poorly in comparison to whites. More than a third (37 percent) of all black families in 1990 had an income under $15,000, while only 14 percent of white families did. Similarly, 32.5 percent of white families received an income of more than $50,000, but only 14.5 percent of black families earned a similar amount. When one considers changes in the distribution of black family income between 1970 and 1990, only one bright spot appears. The percentage of black families earning more than $50,000 per year grew from 9.9 percent to 14.5 percent. It is significant, however, that the percentage of black families earning less than $15,000 actually increased from 34.6 percent in 1970 to 37 percent in 1990.

Another disturbing trend is reflected in the fact that within the black population there is an increasing inequality in the distribution of income. Between 1978 and 1988, the average income of the bottom fifth of black families declined by 24 percent, while the income of the top 5 percent of black families grew by 24 percent. By 1990, the top 5 percent of black families received almost half (47 percent) of total black income.

## Jobs

In his book *Savage Inequalities,* Jonathan Kozol writes that North Lawndale, a neighborhood in Chicago, has one bank, a single supermarket, 99 licensed bars, and 48 state lottery agents. Fifty-eight percent of the men and women 17 years and older are unemployed. Between 1960 and 1970, North Lawndale lost 75 percent of its businesses and 25 percent of its jobs. During the following decade, 80 percent of the remaining manufacturing jobs were lost. The corporations that left included Sears, International Harvester, Sunbeam, and Western Electric.[20]

The neighborhood that Kozol describes is indicative of the economic plight of the American inner city in the 1990s: high unemployment, no investment

---

[20] Jonathan Kozol, *Savage Inequalities* (New York: Crown, 1991).

capital, few manufacturing jobs, and boarded up businesses. The black unemployment rate nationally is almost three times as high as the white rate (11 percent for blacks versus 4 percent for whites). Further, it is estimated that 30 percent of the millions of "discouraged workers" who have given up looking for jobs are also black. The statistics are particularly bleak for young blacks. In New York City, less than one out of 10 black youths aged 16 to 19 have a job. Nationally, the proportion of black male high school dropouts aged 20 to 24 who have not worked at all during the past year climbed from 15 percent in 1974 to 42 percent in 1996. The corresponding proportions for young white dropouts were only 9 percent in 1974 and 15 percent in 1996, while for Hispanics the figures were 9 percent and 11 percent. For black high school dropouts, real annual income declined by an astounding 50 percent between 1973 and 1989. In part, the high unemployment rates and corresponding declines in income can be attributed to the loss of manufacturing jobs. The nation lost 3 million such jobs between 1979 and 1991. In Cleveland, 37 percent of the manufacturing jobs have been lost since 1979.

This dismal employment picture for young, poorly educated blacks is balanced by the success enjoyed by middle-class blacks. In 1940, less than 200 thousand blacks held white-collar jobs. Significantly, 100 thousand of them were teachers, clergymen, and small businessmen. By 1990, almost 2 million blacks were employed in professional and managerial positions. During 1950 to 1990, the black population doubled, but the number of blacks employed in white-collar positions rose by almost 1000 percent. Many of these black professionals are employed by the government. For example, 30 percent of black scientists and more than 33 percent of black lawyers are employed by government agencies. Blacks also account for 20 percent of all jobs in the U.S. Postal Service. The heavy reliance of the black middle class upon government jobs has proven to be a mixed blessing. Given recent budget cuts and the decline in government hiring, the average incomes of black college men dropped by 11 percent between 1979 and 1989. However, the average incomes of white college men grew by the same percentage, reflecting their greater reliance upon a growing private sector during that same period.

One widely recognized cause of high unemployment among blacks living in the central city is the transformation from an industrial/manufacturing economy to one that emphasizes service production and information processing. In a related vein, many businesses have also relocated from the central city to the suburbs. These trends have been particularly devastating for young, poorly educated inner-city blacks. Earlier waves of immigrants to the city were able to take advantage of the numerous jobs generated by an economy based on the production and distribution of manufactured goods. These jobs generally required manual skills rather than sophisticated training. Protected by a robust economy and powerful labor unions, these jobs guaranteed both good pay and economic security. They provided the basis for home ownership, cars, education of the children, and a secure retirement. Both stable families and stable neighborhoods flourished in such an environment.

The manufacturing base has been seriously eroded in many central cities. In New York, for example, 492 thousand jobs requiring less than a high school education were lost between 1970 and 1984. Similarly, 172 thousand such jobs were lost in Boston, and another 89 thousand disappeared in St. Louis. Significantly, however, New York gained 239 thousand jobs during the same period that required some higher education.[21]

Jobs requiring relatively low skill and educational levels have by no means disappeared from the American economy. In fact, more than 2 million such jobs were created in the food and drink industry alone between 1975 and 1985. However, almost all of these new jobs were located in suburban and nonmetropolitan areas. Consequently, they were of no help to the inner-city unemployed.

Unfortunately, the declining availability of entry level jobs in the central city has coincided with a number of other trends that have exerted a negative impact upon the employment prospects of blacks. First, the national economy can no longer be expected to grow at a steady rate. Instead, the experience of the past two decades suggests a cyclical pattern of growth, stagnation, and recession. In such an unpredictable economic environment, poor blacks are the "last to be hired, first to be fired." A second factor has been the entry of millions of women and immigrants into the workforce. These new applicants have significantly increased the competition for entry-level jobs. Third, the national government is deeply in debt. Consequently, both federal spending and hiring are depressed. Finally, the new economic system rewards advanced educational training. Unfortunately, there is little evidence to suggest that blacks are educationally prepared to take advantage of these employment opportunities. For example, 25 percent of whites aged 25 to 34 have college degrees. However, only 13 percent of blacks aged 25 to 34 have college degrees. From 1976 to 1988, the percentage of whites aged 18 to 24 enrolled in college increased from 27 percent to 31 percent. However, the percentage of blacks in this age group enrolled in college actually dropped from 23 percent to 21 percent. Jonathan Kozol's description of a kindergarten class in Chicago offers a bleak assessment of the future for an entire generation of young blacks. He writes that,

> Twelve years from now . . . 14 of these 23 boys and girls will have dropped out of school. Fourteen years from now, four of these kids, at most, will go to college. Eighteen years from now, one of those four may graduate from college, but three of the twelve boys in the kindergarten will already have spent time in

---

[21] John D. Kasarda, "The Regional and Urban Redistribution of People and Jobs in the U.S." Paper prepared for the National Research Council Committee on National Urban Policy, 1986.

prison. If one stands here in this kindergarten room and does not know these things, the moment seems auspicious. But if one knows the future that awaits them, it is terrible to see their eyes look up at you with friendliness and trust—to see this and to know what is in store for them.[22]

It was not always this way. At the turn of the century, a larger proportion of urban blacks than whites were employed. This could be attributed in significant part to the fact that many fewer black women gave up their jobs after marriage. In Philadelphia, black women gave birth to 30 percent fewer children than white women. Murder rates among blacks were lower than those among the immigrant Irish, and medical records suggest that blacks experienced fewer problems with alcohol than whites. A well-organized network of community organizations provided a substantial measure of economic as well as social support. Churches, mutual-aid, and self-help organizations provided health, insurance, and death benefits. The membership in many of these organizations cut across class lines since the black middle and working classes lived in close proximity to each other.

However, several developments during the coming decades would profoundly alter the course of black economic and educational progress. Racism played a crucial role. Blacks who graduated from college and professional schools couldn't earn a living. Whites shunned their services and other blacks couldn't afford to hire them. In the early part of the twentieth century, for example, not a single black attorney in Philadelphia could make a living at his profession. Blacks were systematically excluded from most occupations and trades. Factory and white collar jobs were reserved for whites. Labor unions barred blacks from membership and white union workers walked off the job site if blacks were hired. As a result, blacks were prevented from serving the apprenticeships crucial to the development of marketable skills. The widespread exclusion of blacks from well-paying jobs in the rapidly growing national economy was reflected in the fact that early in this century in Philadelphia 76 percent of blacks worked as "unskilled labor" or were employed in "personal and domestic service." However, only 28 percent of white immigrants and only 12 percent of native-born whites worked in these job categories. On the other hand, 47 percent of white immigrants and 40 percent of native-born whites had manufacturing jobs. Only 8 percent of blacks were similarly employed.

Black Americans emerged from the slave era with an intact family structure, strong work habits, and a belief in the value of education. It was racism and the attendant lack of educational and employment opportunities that created the poverty cycle and the black underclass.

---

[22] Kozol, *Savage Inequalities*.

### White Myths/Black Truths

*Myth:* Blacks are lazier than whites and blacks are more likely to prefer welfare to working.

*Fact:* A higher proportion of black men than white men were employed in the workforce from 1890 until after World War II, and black females were more likely than white females to be employed until 1990. Even young black men—aged 20 to 24 years old—were more likely than white men in the same age category to be employed until 20 years ago. Even now the employment levels of black and white females are almost the same, and black male employment rates are only slightly lower than those of white men (69.5 percent versus 76.4 percent). The major differential that does exist is found for teenagers. Only 35.4 percent of black teenagers have a job as compared to 56 percent of white teens.

*Myth:* Blacks are no longer discriminated against in terms of housing and jobs.

*Fact:* A study conducted in 1994 found that real estate agents discriminated against blacks at least half of the time by showing them fewer rental units than shown to white clients, and by steering them to houses and apartments located in black neighborhoods. The Federal Reserve Board found that in 1992 black applicants were twice as likely to be denied a mortgage loan as whites, even when their economic situations were similar. Other studies have shown that when the proportion of black families in a neighborhood exceeds approximately 10 percent, white residents will begin to move out and others will not buy homes there. With respect to employment, one research project used black and white male college students to apply for several hundred entry-level jobs in Washington, DC, and Chicago. The students were picked so that blacks and whites were equally matched with respect to qualifications for the position. Significantly, one out of every five white students experienced greater success in the application process than their black counterparts.

*Myth:* Blacks hold highly negative views of the police.

*Fact:* Both blacks and whites are highly favorable in their evaluation of the police. Eighty-five percent of blacks believe that the police do a good or fair job of fighting crime, compared to 90 percent of whites.

Plagued by crime, violence, drugs, soaring unemployment, poverty, and welfare dependency, there is little evidence to suggest that conditions will significantly improve in the near future for blacks in the inner city. Many whites think government has done enough, and many others believe it has done too much already. The problems of race and the city rank low on the national political agenda. Even if the will to do something were present in the high councils of government, the huge national debt makes concerted action politically unfeasible. Many Americans, including some blacks, seriously doubt that more

**TABLE 6.4**  Families Receiving Aid for Dependent Children

| Race | Percent | How Long on AFDC | Percent |
|---|---|---|---|
| White | 38.8 | Less than 7 months | 18.2 |
| Black | 39.8 | 7 to 12 months | 13.2 |
| Hispanic | 15.7 | 1 to 2 years | 17.3 |
| Asian | 2.4 | 2 to 5 years | 26.3 |
| Other | 3.3 | Over 5 years | 25.0 |

*Source:* Andrew Hacker, *Two Nations* (New York: Scribners, 1992).

federal spending and programs would make any difference. Instead, they maintain that the federal welfare system itself is responsible for high black unemployment and the breakdown of the black family. Others argue that the changing economy and the loss of manufacturing jobs in the central city are responsible for the black plight. Still others attribute the social and economic isolation of inner-city black neighborhoods to the escape of the black middle class.

Unfortunately, no matter how compelling these explanations are on their merits, none of them offers a solution. The huge problems of race and poverty in the city remain as serious, and as apparently intractable today as they were a quarter-of-a-century ago (Table 6.4).

## HISPANICS

> It is no accident that these regions have the names they do: Los Angeles, San Antonio, San Francisco, Colorado, Montana. The people who built this area in the first place were Hispanics.
>
> Henry Cisneros,
> Secretary of Housing and Urban Development

There are more than 24 million Hispanics in the United States. Further, their rapid growth suggests that they have the potential to become a major force in American politics. The U.S. Census Bureau estimates that the Hispanic population will surpass the black population by the year 2013. Projections indicate that in 20 years there will be more than 42 million Hispanics in the nation. While the black population will grow from 32 million today to 62 million in 2050, the number of Hispanics will increase to 50 million in 2020 and 81 million in 2050. Hispanics will account for more than 40 percent of the nation's population growth during the next 60 years. Hispanics will constitute the nation's largest racial minority in two decades.